What people are saying about…

# OVERCOMING *Mediocrity* ©

5 out of 5 Stars

Inspirational!

*"We all have a story and each one of these is unique and amazing in their own way. I finished a chapter and couldn't wait to read the next story."*

—Roger

5 out of 5 Stars

Fearlessly and Wonderfully Made

*"This book is so encouraging and uplifting, that I couldn't put it down. I originally got this book to support one of my dear friends but quickly fell in love with every story that I read. The encouragement that came from every story hit home in every aspect of my life. I'm so grateful something like this was written. The younger generation definitely needs to hear stories and successful stories of women that suffer through some hard times and come out victorious!!"*

—Eden

5 out of 5 Stars

Expand Your Life! Read This Book!

*"This book is an inspiration. It is worth reading just to see what so-called "average" women can do in their "everyday" lives."*

—Doc

5 out of 5 Stars

It is a Great Investment in Yourself

*"This is an inspiring compilation. Each woman's story contains powerful lessons that are widely applicable. They are heartwarming and triumphant all at the same time. Any woman who's tread a rocky path on her life's journey will be able to relate and rejoice along with each author as she overcomes adversity and challenge. If you're seeking inspiration to overcome adversity, take a moment to breathe, regroup and soak up a story or three. It's a great investment in yourself."*

—Debbra

5 out of 5 Stars

Inspired, Raw Stories from the Heart

*"Inspiring! As someone who cares about helping people in a purposeful way, I continually find myself reminded that everyone has a story. Through raw sharing, they willingly own their history-no easy feat! I highly recommend this book for any woman who is looking for support, another way, or camaraderie and who may struggle in her own path; someone who finds inspiration from others who have overcome often great challenges and have paved the way for the rest of us. There is a difference between mediocrity and adversity. These authors have set the bar to overcome both. Kudos to all."*

— Brenda

5 out of 5 Stars

Highly Recommend!!

*"HIGHLY RECOMMEND!!! If you are looking for personal and professional development, this book is for you! It is perfectly inspiring, educational, empowering and beautifully written! I could really relate to the struggles in their personal stories. It has helped me to continue working on overcoming my own obstacles, so I can succeed in life and in business! Thank you all for sharing your incredible journeys."*

—Lisa

5 out of 5 Stars

Excellent Read for Men and Women!

*"LOVED THE BOOK! [Husband] thought it should not be limited to a "women's" book—excellent for men and women. Writing was personal, intimate, yet clearly educational in nature. Long enough to take you somewhere, but short enough to sit down and read right then. The book is downloaded on our Kindle, so we can read again."*

—TJ

What our clients are saying about...

# OVERCOMING
## *Mediocrity*©

"*I'm passionate about helping women overcome the lies that are holding them back. The problem was that I still believed my own lies. I questioned if my story could actually make a difference, feared that no one would want to hear it and didn't trust I could write it well enough for it to be published. Until I met Christie. She invited me to share my story in one of her books, and it completely transformed my business, my life and best of all, the lives of the women who read it. They've reached out to me, grateful for how what I shared helped them overcome their adversities. Hearing those women's testimonies gave me confidence and fueled me to keep writing. With Christie's help, I published my own book just a few months later, and am currently writing the next in that series.*"

—Shannon Ferraby
Author, Speaker and Trainer with Success Unwrapped
*Overcoming Mediocrity Influential Women*

"*Working with Christie and her team was just the nudge I needed to finally sit down and start writing. The social media tips that were provided when the book launched were also invaluable for engaging and re-engaging people who follow me. I am much more confident about my next book, and it's launch.*"

—Valerie Mrak
Speaker • Filmmaker • Storyteller • Coach
*Overcoming Mediocrity Victorious Women*

"I am an Amazon Best Selling Author! How cool is that? Just to let you know, there are more people than my mother and myself that care about that. It makes a difference to my clients!

Being an author in the series has opened doors for me. It makes it easier to rise to the top of the list for those responsible for booking speaking gigs to want to talk to me. The traffic to my website and Business Page has increased measurably. It has shortened the know, like, trust factor. People are reaching out to me first, before I reach out to them. The titles of the books help women who want to stretch themselves. Who wouldn't want to associate themselves and work with an author who is Dynamic, Resilient, Strong and Influential?"

—Jeanne Lyons
Career Breakthrough Coach
*Overcoming Mediocrity Influential Women*

"My motto is, if you are not having fun, you are doing something wrong. Christie and the DPWN Team made the publishing process so seamless and, dare I say fun because they have created a system that is working. All I had to do was to follow the bouncing smiley face (not literally of course).

When I learned about this project, I was already fully into the writing, publishing and marketing process of my other book, Getting Yourself Unstuck. However, I couldn't put everything in that book. Therefore, Overcoming Mediocrity allowed me to publish a very personal story that didn't seem to fit in my other book. Now going forward in my marketing, the two books will work in tandem."

—Angie Engstrom
Coach and Plank Trainer
*Overcoming Mediocrity Resilient Women*

*"Christie and the OM team took an overwhelming and complicated process of book publishing and made it very easy to get my story published. I was guided through the process from start to finish. Every detail was outlined, and my questions were always answered promptly. The book has received rave reviews, and it has taken my credibility to the next level, as I am now an Amazon #1 best seller! Thank you!!"*

—Lynn O'Dowd
Motivational Speaker and Keynote Performer
*Overcoming Mediocrity Influential Women*

# *Overcoming Mediocrity*

# Other Overcoming Mediocrity Titles

Overcoming Mediocrity - Dynamic Women

Overcoming Mediocrity - Courageous Women

Overcoming Mediocrity - Strong Women

Overcoming Mediocrity - Remarkable Women

Overcoming Mediocrity - Resilient Women

Overcoming Mediocrity - Influential Women

Overcoming Mediocrity - Victorious Women

Overcoming Mediocrity - Fearless Women

# UNSTOPPABLE WOMEN

# OVERCOMING
## *Mediocrity*©

**A unique collection of stories from unstoppable women who have created their own lives of significance!**

Presented by Christie L. Ruffino

## DPWN Publishing

www.OvercomingMediocrity.org

For more information, contact:
DPWN Publishing
A division of the Dynamic Professional Women's Network, Inc.
1879 N. Neltnor Blvd. #316, West Chicago, IL 60185
www.OvercomingMediocrity.org
www.OurDPWN.com

Printed in the United States of America

ISBN: 978-1-939794-19-2

# Dedication

This book is dedicated to the unstoppable women, who faced and overcame challenging times during such an unprecedented time in human history; the 2020 COVID-19 epidemic.

A special dedication to the most UNSTOPPABLE woman in my life, Susan Jean Giannini (Crowley). Sue was my best friend, my confidant, my advisor, my encourager, my number one fan and my mom. Although she couldn't overcome the debilitating physical conditions that plagued her final years, she demonstrated courage and sheer unstoppable-ness during every aspect of her life, until the very end.

You can read her story at www.MyLegacyJournal.com/Sue

# The Power of a Story

There is nothing more important in this world than the relationships we build and the legacy we leave in the lives of those who've crossed paths with us on our journey of life. It's the experiences we have during this journey that define our individual uniqueness and create our own powerful personal blueprint or our unique story snowflake.

It is this blueprint that can empower and equip us to possess a distinct advantage over every other person in this world, if leveraged correctly and shared. If we don't have the courage to share our snowflake, it will be lost forever. No one will have the same story, and no one can repeat your story. Therefore, those who come after you will never learn anything from what you've experienced and what you've learned.

I feel that the most significant thing we can do to add value back to this world, is to master the narrative of our lives. All of our leadership and moneymaking abilities rest in our ability to discover, craft and deliver our personal story or message in a way that will allow people to connect to us. The right story shared at the right time with the right person can alter the trajectory of their life, as well as our own.

We can also learn from other people's stories to change the direction of our own story and redirect our ultimate destiny.

Power to you and the story of your life!

*"Individually we're strong; together, we're unstoppable!"*

—Christie Ruffino

# Introduction

When I embarked upon this journey, never in my wildest dreams did I expect it to turn out as it has. My motives were grand, yet much more simplistic than they are today.

My initial goal was to create one co-authored book, collecting stories from women I admired who were members of my organization, the Dynamic Professional Women's Network (DPWN). I knew how sharing my story in a similar book (compiled by a mentor of mine, Michelle Prince) had been transformational for me. I also knew how having a book to share in the business community gave me additional credibility, recognition and exposure. What I didn't know was how these same stories would be just as transformational for the readers, as they related to one or more of the women who were willing to share their stories in such a vulnerable and authentic way.

I also had no way of knowing how working with these women would lead me down a path that would change 'my' life forever…

**My Story**

I'm a natural connector. Many women are. I believe that it is a part of our DNA to connect people with other people or resources that can help them. Many times, I've shared how my journey to build DPWN was not intentional. As an introvert, the last thing I wanted to do was build a business where I would have to frequently talk with new people… strangers. However, thankfully, God knew better than I did what was best for me.

Now, 17 years later, our community is thriving in the Chicagoland area, and we've also expanded globally. We have a fierce online presence with virtual meetings, on-demand training and Mastermind Success Circles. You can connect with us at www.OurDPWN.com.

Personally, I work with women who are on a quest to build a profitable and impactful business as a coach, author and speaker. That's my passion and where my story has brought me thus far. I'm blessed to wake up every day, knowing that I can help my clients live into THEIR passion; which is to help their clients. We're creating a wonderful ripple effect. You can connect with me at www.ChristieRuffino.com.

Our *Overcoming Mediocrity Project* is going just as strong, celebrating book number nine featuring an amazing lineup of unstoppable women and a brand-new Podcast. The stories in each of our books are about strength, faith and courage. They are about having the confidence to believe in ourselves, even when those we love may not. They're about having the courage to do hard things, even when we don't want to. They are also about remaining unstoppable through all of life's ups and downs because that is what, as women, we do brilliantly. Do you have a story of strength, faith, or courage? You can connect with us at www.overcomingmediocrity.org.

**Your Story**

What is your story? ARE YOU LIVING YOUR STORY? Or are you living for someone else's story? Maybe you ARE living into your destiny. Or maybe you spend the majority of your time unhappily working for someone else, taking care of someone else, or doing something that does not create a fire in your soul. You're managing, thinking… one of these days it will be my turn. What if that time never comes?

The personal and professional development industry generates billions of dollars of revenue every year. According to www.marketresearch.com, the estimated market value for personal coaching in the United States was $955 million in 2015 and $1.02 billion in 2016. This market value is expected to reach $1.34 billion by 2022, which is a 6.7% average yearly growth rate.

The great news is that for every one of those coaches, there are countless people desperately searching for help.

I work with women who have reached a point in their lives where they're finally ready to step into their destiny, own their story and share their wisdom. There are women who don't think they have the skills to become a coach, but they know down deep in their gut that they can help people. They're considering stepping into a coaching or consulting role, but they don't know where to start, or they've been trying and they're just not getting the results they desire (or frankly that they deserve).

If you just read that and felt a butterfly or two swirling around in your stomach, then maybe we should chat. I have a simple system that will provide you with the steps and support to build a profitable business as a coach, author and speaker.

You can learn more at www.CreateSuccessWithChristie.com.

## Our Books — Their Story

Our first *Overcoming Mediocrity* book was a smashing success! On the very first day of its release in 2013, it became the #1 downloaded Kindle book in the motivational genre category. Twenty-two women shared their stories to inspire other women to overcome and succeed as they had, and all authors were able to claim the distinguished Amazon Bestselling Author status.

Because of the overwhelming success of that first book, we went on to produce additional books under the *Overcoming Mediocrity* brand. Each of them also climbed to the #1 position on Amazon on the very first day of release. Three of them, *Overcoming Mediocrity — Resilient Women*, *Influential Women* and *Fearless Women*, all reached the #1 position in two categories, which was a great accomplishment.

These books have ultimately taken on a life of their own and have made a greater impact than ever anticipated. It is exciting to read testimonials from women who have read and connected with one or more of the inspirational stories inside. It's even more exciting when one of those same women decide to share their story in one of our future books.

It is now with great honor and pride that I can share stories from the unstoppable women in this book. I've had the pleasure of getting to know each of these ladies and learning a little about the stories they're sharing with you. I'm deeply inspired by the courage they're exhibiting. They are sharing the personal details of their lives with the sole intention of allowing you, the reader, to learn from their experiences and wisdom.

It's easy to become complacent. You can live a life of mediocrity, just coasting through day by day. It takes courage to fight through the hard and overcome challenges that seem impossible to defeat. The women in the pages of this book made a purposeful choice to live significant lives and share their stories to help you also live a life of significance. This demonstrates strength, humility and the heart of a true go-giver. These women all have even greater things yet to come. They are women whom you should know, learn from and emulate.

This book is meant to not only encourage you but to also awaken your inner desire to share your story along with them. Each woman in our project wants to make the biggest possible impact in the world and transform as many lives as possible, by sharing their story and wisdom in a book that will get massive exposure. They could have kept their stories private. That would have been the safest and easiest path for them. However, they decided to step out of their comfort zone and share the narratives of their lives with you. We invite you to join them on this journey.

I am blessed to have the opportunity to share these UNSTOPPABLE women with you. I hope that you feel just as blessed to receive the value they offer you.

If you'd like more information about joining our project, visit www.OvercomingMediocrity.org.

Hugs & Blessings,

Christie

# Table of Contents

# Regina Young

## *Standing in Your Own Power*

No guts. No glory. No tests. No story. I was always an independent thinker. As I looked around my apartment in Philadelphia, I realized when I decided to be the author of my life and my choices, which brings me to this moment in midlife.

**First**

I felt that to move forward into the next phase of my journey, I had to take ownership of my past choices; the good, the bad and the ugly. There is no value dragging forward the past choices that no longer serve me. By recognizing those decisions, I choose not to repeat old patterns. I needed to give up the comfort zone, for what has been the opportunity to be authentically me.

While working with a network marketing company, I met a sharp young man, who knew how to lead a team and had personal power. I asked him, "How did he develop himself like that?" He said, "The Forum." That was the end of the conversation.

I knew that I did not want to go through life after divorce, without any sort of support. I wanted ME back, after being someone's girlfriend, wife and partner for 12 years. So, I looked up The Forum. When I went online to research The Forum, this "transformational leadership course", as the website stated, would take place over a weekend and an evening. Coincidentally, the location of the course was nearby at a hotel around the corner from my job at *People Magazine*.

The next evening when I went, what I heard caught me off guard. It was a "completion evening" for people who just finished the Forum and their guests. Even though I didn't know anyone there, I felt comfortable. People were standing up at the microphone sharing their hearts out, on how their life would never be the same for themselves and the people in their lives. I was touched by their authenticity.

There was one guy who stood up and started to tell my story. He shared that he was the cause for his divorce. He admitted he was controlling and afraid that he was going to lose his wife, because she had no space to be his partner. He told his ex-wife that he was sorry and promised to be a better co-parenting partner for their kids. He asked his ex-wife to stand up. Everyone clapped, as we wiped away tears.

It was clear. He was owning his role in the failure of his marriage. He was freed up by not feeling guilty and he was straight about everything he did that did not work. That was my story on the other side of divorce and the impact it would have on my life.

The course was the difference-maker for him. I had wanted to put all the blame on our failed marriage on my ex-husband. That's when I knew that this course was what I wanted for me and my life. So, I signed up that evening.

Two weeks later, I was in the course unpacking old decisions and choices I made as a child that no longer served me now as an adult. I began to feel a freedom to create a life that would be fulfilling, alive and authentic, by letting go of the old disappointments. We had dated for four years and were married for eight.

I had to own that I chose to compromise myself, by giving my power away. Eventually I felt abandoned, because I was not getting as much as I was giving. By demanding his attention, I did not see how it was diminishing his spirit. I was not speaking to him from my heart, just my head.

I accepted that we had stopped being a team and that our dreams had died at the end of the marriage. I went back to my ex-husband and said that I was sorry that it didn't work out. I took ownership of my 'Demanding Delilah' ways. Before the course, I wanted to be right and get my pound of flesh out of my ex-husband. Since finishing the course, I was clear why we grew apart. I learned that I could leave him in a most loving way, without destroying him on the way out of our marriage. I just chose to leave him with love. I learned that being true to myself and owning my part of what did not work in my marriage, would empower me moving forward in my life. I recognized that my self-limiting beliefs held me back from sharing and creating a powerful relationship. The sense of freedom to be able to make choices with love and compassion for myself, and how I treat others, leaves me unstoppable.

**Second**

While visiting New York for an open-call at a modeling agency, I felt confident in my skin as a full-figured woman of color. I knew that I was tall enough and besides that, I was photogenic. As I entered the building of the modeling agency, the guard directed me to take the elevator. I was to get off at the top floor, and then walk up the stairs to the penthouse. The stairs opened up to the agency room, with chairs lined up on both sides of the wall. There was only one handful of girls hoping to see if the agency would be interested in representing them as new models. Open calls were held once a week, so wannabees and more other experienced models went to the audition to find representation in the fashion industry.

Finally, it was my turn with the talent agent. I was a little scared, as she asked me to walk down an aisle like a runway and turn, then walk towards her. "You have a very pretty face. I would represent you, if you get a nose job and lost 20 pounds." I knew that I was not the picture of a typical super model, but I did not need *that* level of overhaul to get into the industry. I left the agency knowing that was not my kind of agency, if I was not enough just the way I am. This agency represented full-figured women, so I found it strange to experience all the judgment I faced.

Deep in my heart, I knew that I did not need to do all that to become a full-figured model.

Without an agency in New York, it was a catch-22. You need an agency to get a job, and a job to get more experience. Without an agency in New York, it's like wandering in the wilderness with no map. Being discovered as a full-figured woman of color was a pipe dream. Another model said it can take up to 15 years to get a break in the New York fashion industry.

I went back to Philadelphia and made up my mind. After I graduated from the Art and Fashion Institute of Philadelphia, I was going to move to the Midwest. I was more determined than ever to break into the fashion industry, no matter what those agencies said.

With no connections, no family and just one friend in town, I moved to Minneapolis and took a leap of faith. If it is to be, it is up to me.

A few months later, in my Minneapolis studio apartment, I realized that I was living my dream. I was a big fish in a little pond. I got an agent and they started sending me to go see about modeling jobs. I booked my first modeling gig with Target. The gigs then fell in line with weekly advertisement circulars and runway shows for department stores, like Dayton Hudson, Donaldson's, Saks Fifth Avenue in the Mall of America and the Twin City Live Morning Show.

Then one evening, after a long day at work, the break came in over my answering machine. It was my agent letting me know that I had been selected to model in a runway show and be in the newspaper advertisement for the New York BBWL's President's book tour. I was very excited, because in that moment I realized that I had made the right choice to move to the Midwest and more importantly, to not listen to that other agency that wanted me to get a nose job. They did not understand that I knew my value and I was just fine the way I was. The local midwestern agency accepted and appreciated me, just for me. Yes, I got to work with the New York agencies' President. She invited me to stop by the agency, the next time I was in the Big Apple. To make a long story short, four months later, I signed a contract with the President of BBWL.

Before you knew it, I was working with Essence, BELLE, BBW Magazine and was on The Kathy Lee and Regis Philbin Show. Three months after that, I became a New York Ford Model.

By listening to my intuition and being determined and unstoppable, only I can define my value. When you look for validation by other sources, outside of yourself, it leads to disappointment and undermines your personal power.

Where are you looking for validation and not being responsible for your beauty and value?

Today, I work as a self-image branding coaching/consultant with my company called, **"ModelPerfect Woman."**

**ModelPerfect Woman** coaches' women on how to create their own unique self-image — polished, poised, and professional.

ModelPerfect Woman is for women either re-entering the labor force or those who want to accept themselves in a new, polished light. Women, of any age, can be stuck in the idea of who they were in their past. They can do this by discovering, redefining and rebranding themselves, while giving up old conversations that block them from seeing their value when they look in the mirror. There is nothing wrong with you right now. You are stuck with a picture of yourself from 10 years ago, when you were younger, 10 lbs. lighter and happy with yourself. ModelPerfect Woman turns the light back on in every woman, so she can see her beauty, value and personal power.

**Third**

When I heard there was a pandemic, it was way further down the line, somewhere like mid-March 2020. It reminded me of SARS and Ebola. They were both pandemics that were highly contagious and originated in another country. I worked in New York City during 9/11, so when the news reporter said, "It was like a silent intruder, living under the constant gloom, doom, and fear of not knowing what was next. It was like the world went through this painful event with us.

Then there was the calm and clarity that occurred in the aftermath and my financial future was in my own hands.

I've always challenged myself in life. When I'm down, I always say, "Learn something new, because when you look up, you'll be in a different space and place." Now with Covid-19, the pandemic shut the world down and suddenly my time was my own again. I called that, "Standing in a clearing." It was a new opportunity to create something big in my life and open conversations that could transform something.

With the world on hold and everyone quarantined at home, I had stumbled into the perfect captive audience. I must thank God, because three months prior to the pandemic, I set myself up strategically by taking a hiatus from the 9–5 world and linked up with a career coach. I had come to the realization that I was putting all my energy and effort into the wrong basket, which was just my job. I began choosing to put my energy into something that was exciting and mine. I had been in conversation about the experiences that women have in midlife with friends. I created podcast episodes that last as long as it takes to drink a cup of your favorite tea. I had already done the work, acquired the equipment and studied YouTube for podcasters. It was like a teenager trying to learn a new dance. I believed that I could do it and I had confidence in my abilities. However, I still had to find a way to cover my expenses. I decided to take money out of my 401K. I knew that I had to live my dream now, not wait until I retired. Let's be honest, who knows how motivated I would be at that point? Nevertheless, I split the money right down the middle, some for now and some for later. I declared that I was worthy of this created opportunity. I had chosen to stop trying to push the ball up the hill, just to have it roll back over and crush me. I'm now grateful that I get to fulfill my dreams.

I've always had a love of tea and appreciation of the midlife transition. Midlife to me is about being in a community with other women, while sharing our victories, struggles and breakdowns, one teacup conversation at a time.

Instead of being isolated, alone with a pet in midlife, Teatime Midlife

Edition Podcast created a community/tribe that could be seen, heard and be unstoppable in midlife.

Teatime Midlife Edition was slated to start May 3, 2020. However, since the pandemic hit, I chose to move up the launch date of my podcast to March 22, 2020. My goal was to provide the people with questions and conversations about choices women could take on in midlife. It is about creating a life of passion, purpose and fun. It involves helping each person discover how they could be the author of the next chapter in their life. For me, this is my opportunity to be vulnerable and authentically me. It gives me a chance to be a living example of what it looks like to be an unstoppable woman in midlife and beyond.

My first podcast was published with the help of a team made up of family and friends. They included a talented branding expert, music producer and photographer. I already had a timeline of the topics I wanted to discuss about midlife and teas. All I had to do was focus and put my energy to create just one podcast to get started. It didn't have to be perfect. I just had to choose to get started.

When you choose to own your risk, getting started is one of many risks you have to take on. However, it gets easier. Because I chose to take this risk in my life, the world gets to experience my journey. What a gift it is to share!

It first started with a choice to stop pushing everything that was not going my way fast enough. I never thought I could be going the wrong way. Life had become about surviving it versus creating my journey. I then started creating the first episodes about myself and my journey that led me to this moment. The second episode talked about standing in a clearing and recognizing, like the pandemic, New Year's and your birthday. It was about getting the opportunity to create whatever you want in your clearing. The third episode was about Standing in a Clearing and Owning It. My guest was on the verge of retiring and starting a life with no structure. Of course, I asked the traditional question, "What are you going to do with all your newfound time?"

She replied with a list. It included photography, painting, poetry and traveling with her husband. It seemed like such an automatic answer. So I asked, "After that what are you going to do, and then after that, what are you going to do and so on. She finally arrived at a space, where she shared that she really wanted to read books to elderly people, like she had done with her mother in her later years. She missed that kind of interaction in her life. I was very moved by her sharing her experience so authentically, from her heart. She was standing in her clearing and owning it.

What is your heart's desire? You know, the thing you said, "I hope to do someday?" If the stars align then I will do that, try this and be that? Yes, that thing. It is the thing that you keep talking yourself out of. Remember that getting started is the first choice, not trying to be perfect, and just taking the risk. Ask yourself the question, "If you knew you could not fail, what would you dare to do?"

Teatime Midlife Edition Podcast can be listened to weekly on Apple, iHeart Radio, Spotify, TuneIn and other major podcast apps.

If you told me a year ago that I would have a podcast in 2020, I would say, "No way!" or "You're joking!" Yet, here we are now. Over 5,000 people, within a month and a half, have been listening to the podcast.

Where in your life are you 'just going through the motions'? Where are you not taking any risks, just living a default life and not owning your excuses, reasons, and comparisons? Are you not giving yourself the credit that you deserve? Your future depends on your choices today.

There are things you can do right now to start your journey and be unstoppable, just by choosing actions that go against what everyone else is doing, being true to yourself and speaking your truth.

I say **own your value**. You don't need the approval of others, if you own your value. Your personal power is in your hands. Know that you are more than enough, and no one can tell you it's not your turn. Know the value you bring versus people telling you your worth. Owning the risk, feeling the fear, doing it anyway.

You never know, you might win in life.

One thing I know to be true is that if you step out on faith, things come together because you are standing in your own power and being unstoppable. You might even surprise yourself and become an Unstoppable Woman.

Takeaways — When did you give up being unstoppable? Who did you allow to turn off your light and devalue you? When and why did you stop taking risks in your life?

I encourage you to define your life's journey in the following ways and stand in your own power.

1. Own Your Stuff — if you know who you are, then owning what works and does not work will give you a choice in your journey.

2. Own Your Value — you define your value because you are enough, and you are worthy. That is personal power.

3. Own the Risk — a life without risk is a life not lived. If it is to be, it is up to me and that is why you take risks.

You can learn more about ModelPerfect Woman at www.modelperfectwoman.com and listen to Teatime Midlife Edition on your favorite streaming podcast app.

# Regina Young

Regina Young has always charted her own journey in life. She has always believed that standing in your own power makes you unstoppable. Regina has a degree from the Art and Fashion Institute of Philadelphia in Fashion. Through perseverance and determination, Regina became a New York Ford Model and Click Model. She could be seen in magazines and advertisements, like ESSENCES, BBW, BELLE and Target. She has also graced the runways of famous department stores, like Saks Fifth Avenue, Nordstrom, Lord and Taylor, Macy's, and Bloomingdales as a full-figured model. Regina developed a passion for being an image consultant for many women transitioning back to work and/or who needed an upgrade of their image to be polished, professional, and ready to take the lead in their life. Working with many women's organizations over the years, like Suited for Success, Bottomless Closet in New York, and The Career Wardrobe in Philadelphia, Regina helped women gain confidence, knowing they looked job-ready. Regina's self -branding image consulting business is called, "ModelPerfect Woman." Regina's podcast Teatime Midlife Edition is a weekly teacup conversation about the victories, challenges, and breakthroughs in the lifestyle of mid-lifers. Her conversations stimulate community with other women, so they can share, develop friendships, and support each other, instead of being isolated and alone in midlife. Every Sunday at 3:00 pm ET, Teatime Midlife Edition Podcast can be found at www.TeatimeMidlifeEdition.com or Apple iTunes, iHeart Podcast, and Spotify apps. For more information about ModelPerfectWoman, check out www.ModelPerfectWoman.com get your free checklist called, "Is It Time To Brand Your Self Image."

Regina Young
ModelPerfect Woman
347-927-8076
YoungRegina2@gmail.com
UnstoppableRegina@gmail.com
www.ModelPerfectWoman.com

# Vicki Parker

## *Parker UnLimited...*

## *...because anything is possible!!!*

What just happened? That's not the conversation I thought I would have today. Here I am in my favorite brightly colored overstuffed chair, completely deflated! I spent the entire morning preparing for this contract negotiation call. I slept a full seven hours, got up early and worked out, spent time in prayer with my devotional and was sure to shower and look smart. How did this happen? I set myself up by having a good breakfast, creating a space of comfort and support all around me. I even washed the dishes, so that everything was clear. I cannot stop staring at my phone as it rests next to my laptop on the TV table in front of me, the words, *"and your last day will be tomorrow!"* repeating over and over in my mind.

Unbeknownst to me, this make-shift executive office is going to be command central in creating what's next for me. My thoughts spin. I replay recent events in my mind. I'm one year into this three-year coaching contract, and 30 minutes ago, on a call with our entire team, it was confirmed that the second year was approved. We wrapped up year-end business and even reviewed travel dates for the upcoming Train-the-Trainer. I can't believe we spent an hour and a half planning a future that's now defunct. After 18 years as an independent contractor with this agency, why did they not provide the professional courtesy of scheduling my performance evaluation before the all-team call? Why even include me? I find myself dumbfounded by the inconsideration and the outcome of this conversation, and yet, somewhat relieved.

After a restless night, I confess to my professional coach, John, "It's true, I have been inconsistent in producing the administrative requirements of the job, but my performance and commitment to the teams I've coached have never waned." "Your performance outcome is one hundred percent correlated with your performance," he says. His keen perception, striking me like a lead balloon. In an effort not to get defensive, I breathe, allowing time for his words to sink in.

Here I am, a performance coach. However, the level of my performance on what I told the company was my "dream job" fell short of my very own professional expectation. It's clear now that I've been playing by my own rules, dismissing the significance the company requires regarding reporting structures. And yet, I resist the communication that I have not executed the contract as designed. I am human. I want to be right about this, but I'm not. That cost me the opportunity for two additional years of consistent work. It's gone. I'm deflated!

"So, what's next," asks my coach. I stare at him, upset with myself for missing the mark. "I guess I need to reach out to my network and…" "No," he interrupts abruptly. Pausing for a moment, "What is performance?" he asks. Biting my lip, I stare at him cluelessly, unable to answer, and asking myself if I understand. I'm holding back the tears, breathing into it, willing myself to be coachable, in-discovery of what there is to learn from all of this. What amazes me, is that as a freelance professional, performing in this arena for 26 years, as a facilitator, trainer, and coach, I cannot even comprehend his question. John asks again, "What is performance?" I have been a coach my entire life! I've choreographed for and coached dancers, gymnasts, actors, automotive professionals, corporate executives and other trainers looking to become coaches. Yet, at this moment, I have no idea how to respond to this question. I'm embarrassed that I can't muster the words and ashamed that I'm failing miserably in my work.

"I dunno," I mumble, blankly.

"All there is to do…," he pauses for emphasis, "…is master performance," he says gently. Kindness, generosity and love overwhelm me. Tears well up in my eyes. As I flounder for words, his reproach, "and there is nothing wrong with you. Who you are is whole, perfect and complete. You simply have insufficient structures in place that are required to achieve your desired performance outcome."

I contemplate his words, with a long, deep breath, allowing them to land in my heart as the tears stream onto my lap. There's nothing wrong with me. I'm perfect the way I am. I'm perfect the way I am not, I repeat each bit like a declaration in my mind. It's my support structures that are insufficient. It is not me, it's my structures. I am a perfect human being, but the framework I've used is not making the grade. A slow smile brightens my tear-streaked face and, with three shallow sighs, of my quivering breath, the tension across my neck and shoulders releases. "Wow, THAT is such a gift," I exclaim! After another deep sigh, I thank him. I am instantly present to the difference it makes to have someone standing for my greatness and coaching me with rigor, love and generosity.

How many times in my life have I missed an opportunity or fallen short of a goal, and made myself wrong for it? I punished myself, as if I were an inept human being, a dreadful individual, or a failure in my personal life, athletic endeavors and business. Then, when this happened, I took myself out of the game for an hour, a day, a week, or entirely. Mind-boggling! I finally get it. Who I am is perfect! The framework I have in place around this particular career move was not adequate to sustain me in being effective.

"So, what's next," he asks? After I repeat my answer, he gives it to me. "All there is to do is master performance!" Master performance…master performance…That is what I have been doing my entire life. I see it! Now the pieces begin to fit together! My life experience has been quite extraordinary. I see where I have been unshakeable and unstoppable my entire life.

Growing up in Garden City, Michigan, a suburb of Detroit, I enjoyed a comfortable life. When I was 8-years old, my aunt, uncle, and cousins came for a visit on their way home to New York from a cross country vacation. They convinced my parents to let me drive with them and fly home on my own two weeks later. Flying in an airplane for the very first time sparked an ember for travel that gave personal meaning to the phrase, "I could have been a gypsy," which I had heard my mother repeat many times. This act of independence, combined with my love for navigating maps and roads during family vacations in our green wood-paneled station wagon, would have quite an impact on my life choices.

From that trip forward until this day, my relationship with our New York relatives has been powerfully strong. I spent two weeks to two months each summer in Rockland County. My uncle, a New York City Police Sergeant, would drive me into the city for a tour and a street vendor hotdog. When I was in my late teens, he would drop me off at the Port Authority Bus Terminal. After trekking around Manhattan, I would get on a bus and make my way back up to Congers. I loved Manhattan and always dreamed of living there. Although that seemed highly unlikely at this point in life, my self- esteem suffered after my parents' divorce. It was a time of grieving, because not only had my Dad left the house, my four brothers did as well. When Jim went off to college, Mike had already joined the Navy. Joe enlisted the year after that, with Dan joining the Army the following year. That left my mom and me alone in the house. However, she was working two jobs. Life shifted dramatically, with most of my social activity disappearing as well. I never did get back to competitive figure skating or tennis but was able to nurture my creative spirit through dance.

One of my earliest dreams was to become a dancer. I envisioned myself living in my mom's native New York, partnering with the likes of Fred Astaire and Gene Kelly. Life for them seemed magical and not at all like the hardship my mom faced growing up in that city. However, at the age of 14, I was disappointed because, after years as a little league cheerleader, I did not make-the-cut for high school cheer or pom! I started comparing myself to others. All the popular pretty girls are on the team, I told myself as insecurity ebbed its way into my being. If I'm not on cheer or pom, how will I fit in? "You can do anything you want to do, be anyone you want to be," my mother encouraged. So, I didn't cry over it, nope, not me. Besides, the people I related to with the most ease were quirky and fun, the ones always hanging out at the top of the ramp by the auditorium. Auditions for the Silent Concepts Mime Company were also coming up in a few days. I wanted to do that, too! As it turned out, I excelled as a mime, traveling with the troupe throughout the state for the next four years. At the same time, I was getting roles in plays and musicals and finally found my place. My people were the theater geeks, band fags and choir queers. I even started dance lessons again while student teaching, to offset the cost.

It has been years since that first audition, with many more that followed. Some went well, and others, well… didn't. Some of my most vivid and cherished memories are dancing with the Subway Dancers for the Detroit Drive arena football team, Dance Detroit, The Detroit Renaissance Dancers and the Michigan Opera Theater. Shoot, I even auditioned once with my friend, for the Rockettes in New York City! We weren't tall enough and we knew that. However, we got out there and gave it a whirl! Life was an adventure, and we were going for it!

Throughout the six years of my college career, while achieving my degree in Dance and Psychology, I worked at a luxury hotel. At the end of my senior year, the Director of Dance announced some exciting news. "We are going to Japan, she told us, smiling from ear-to-ear. Marygrove College and Dance Detroit, have been invited to participate in a cultural exchange with L' Etoile Ballet in Nagoya, Japan." I simply regarded this as a missed opportunity. There was no way I'd be able to go. In addition to a full load of classes, I was working full-time at the hotel. And that tooth that broke off a few months ago, set me back $1400. It literally caused me to beg my way into school for my final semester on a payment plan. I asked my dad if I could borrow the money for the dental repair, but it was not a possibility. As a matter of principle, my stepmom did not want him to loan money out to his kids, because she feared we would never pay it back. It didn't make sense to me, but when you have a blended family of eight, I suppose boundaries are necessary. This situation was one of them. I never questioned my dad about it. I simply became compliant, never asking again. An adventure in Japan for me, not likely!

In the meantime, the Detroit area was experiencing cultural expansion. Mazda Motor Corporation had recently linked arms with Ford Motor Company, practically on the doorstep of the hotel. This venture had the sales department vying for feasible opportunities to attract Japanese guests to the property. I learned through a co-worker that the hotel would be creating an exchange program with a property in Tokyo to help our sales department connect with the Japanese market. My boss noticed that I was already having fun communicating with our Japanese guests through small phrases I learned from an English/Japanese dictionary that someone left at the front desk. He called me into his office and asked what my plans were after graduation. I told him I was thinking about the Managerial Training Program offered by the hotel. "Oh," he paused, "we would like you to represent our hotel as the Cultural Exchange Ambassador in Tokyo." This was a very awkward exchange, because I knew my colleague had his heart set on that position. After making my boss aware of my concern, he said, "Yeah, you're right, something better will come along for you," which triggered a knee-jerk response. "What do you mean something better will come along for me?" I asked. "What could be better than the opportunity to live in a foreign country, learning the language, customs and culture, earning a paycheck and knowing there's a paid flight home at the end of it all?" He smiled, asking coyly, "Does this mean you'll go?" What synchronicity!!! Vicki Parker, 26 years old from little known Garden City, still gets to go to Japan! I was giddy with excitement and anticipation. In front of me, was an opportunity of a lifetime, and I knew it!

I experienced eight magnificent months in Japan, filled with the excitement of learning and the challenge of adapting to a society that had been closed off from the world for many years. I found the culture intriguing and not predictable by American standards. The people I came to know had a yearning to understand the American mindset, and I discovered fast friends in people from all over the world. I experienced kindness, love, trust and generosity in many wonderful relationships with the time passing far too quickly. Anticipating this adventure would land me in a position of importance within the corporation, I also looked forward to sharing the knowledge I acquired with the managerial team back home. To my dismay, not one colleague was even remotely interested. And although I became the Concierge Manager for more than 800 rooms upon my return, it became a position of mediocrity for me over the next four years. The hotel was no longer operating at a premium level, luxury and opulence aside, the experience for our guests paralleled that of our staff as our offerings gradually diminished.

Then one day, a well-mannered bellman that I had known for at least a decade, asked in all sincerity, "Vicki, what are you still doing here?" I was stunned by the candor he used, as he continued, "You have so much going for you. Why are you allowing this place to take the life out of you?" And just like that, he summed it up. The position no longer served me, because I was no longer vested. This job of twelve years and my-own gypsy dreams thrust me toward the future. It was time to move on, to find my way and to be who I want to be. His prodding was exactly what was needed for me to consider what presented itself next.

When a friend from college said, "They're looking for people who are good with people, and who's more engaging than you?" I released myself from the complacency created by the stability of benefits and steady pay toward a new beginning. This opportunity paved the way for what has become a twenty-six-year adventure as a freelance facilitator in the automotive industry. From national spokesperson on the Auto Show floor to subject matter expert, facilitator, trainer and coach, this career has carried me to all 50 United States and afforded many holidays abroad. That leap of faith not only increased my income substantially, but it also elevated my gypsy dreams to a lifestyle. I have yet to live in New York, but who knows what the future holds? I have been quite content in Chicago, where I have lived in one of the most culturally diverse communities for more than 25 years. As it happens, however, some of my closest friends live in New York City, their generosity affording me the privilege of enjoying the Big Apple experience for days or weeks at a time.

"Master performance Vicki," John says one more time, snapping me back to the present conversation. Without a second thought, I am propelled with terminal velocity, using the pause created by the pandemic to be more unstoppable than ever before. At a time when people are complaining that there is nothing to do, I've been busier than ever, successfully pivoting my business from my executive office at home.

### #WhatHasVickiParkerLearned?

I've learned the significance of technology in bringing together all aspects of my life. It's not just for business. From virtual dance parties and karaoke, to family game nights and working out three times a week with my 85-year-old mother. I've reinforced relationships with many friends and family thanks to Zoom. Virtual summer camp for kids with neuromuscular disease would have been impossible without technology during the COVID pandemic. www.campstrong2020.weebly.com I'm so proud of that accomplishment.

When it comes to my professional life, I envisioned where I want to be with my career as a business owner/investor, accomplished writer and speaker, facilitator and coach. I identified opportunities to refine my abilities, completing five training and coaching courses within a six-month timeframe. I achieved certification to expand my Rodan + Fields skincare business to include the Japanese market https://vickiparker.myrandf.com. I have become a Certified B.A.N.K. IOS Coach, coaching the B.A.N.K. Six Intelligences https://bit.ly/BankOnVicki. I began exploring iPEC's Education system, completing the Life and Leadership Potentials Training Program. I've also completed a Speaker/Coach Sales Training Course with Eric Lofholm as well as a year-long Team, Management, and Leadership Program, with Landmark

Worldwide. I returned to face-to-face Customer Experience coaching for a premium automotive brand. I was a featured speaker during the "Startup In the Gig Economy," Video Summit https://startupinthegigeconomy.org/vicki-parker/. I also expanded my technological skill set, by producing a series of Diversity and Inclusion webinars via Zoom.

As a way of mastering performance, at the onset of a global pandemic, with fear as the underlying current in our world, I began to add layers to the sturdy foundation I've already set. I reinforced the structures that make me prominent in my field. I'm now more capable than ever of making the kind of difference in the world I have so longed to create. I've found that when something doesn't work out according to plan, a great way to reclaim power is to be willing to create what's next.

**The Parker Method**

1. Recognize where you are and how you feel about it.

2. Envision where you want to be and how you want to feel.

3. Back-cast from that vision. (Decide what's necessary to close the gap between where you want to be and where you are).

4. Create opportunities that move you into action.

## Vicki Parker

Vicki Parker, a Detroit native, resides in Chicago. She is an author, keynote Speaker and executive coach. She holds a BFA in Dance and Psychology, is adept at working with teams and teamwork and is known for keeping teams together during times of change and uncertainty. Vicki has an extensive automotive background, is a subject matter expert and coaches top tier automotive brands on elevating the customer experience. Parker is a Certified B.A.N.K. IOS Coach, conducting group and 1:1 coaching of the B.A.N.K. Six Intelligences to enhance communication in selling environments. She believes in generating multiple streams of income, is a real estate investor and an Executive Consultant and CEO of her own Rodan + Fields Skincare business. She exemplifies the true essence of an entrepreneurial spirit. Vicki's breath comes through her relationships and partnering to have others experience being loved, seen and known in our world with a powerful sense of belonging. She is a long-time volunteer with the Muscular Dystrophy Association of Southeastern Michigan, President of the Association for the Physically Challenged and on the Board of Directors for A Mission of Hope. While Vicki doesn't have children of her own, she has impacted the lives of many children with the MDA, Special Olympics, Royal Family Kids Camp, Plan USA, Compassion International and through her philanthropic work in Arts and Education. Vicki loves adventure, travel, experiencing new cultures, cuisines and finds her greatest joy being with her family and friends. Vicki's vision for our world: ALL PEOPLE EMBRACING ONE ANOTHER AS BEST FRIENDS!!! Everywhere is on her bucket list and everyone is on her love list. Parker UnLimited... ...*because anything is possible!!!*

Vicki Parker

Parker UnLimited... ...*because anything is possible!!!*

4536 N. Sheridan Road, Suite 103

Chicago, IL 60640

773-255-3522

UnstoppableVicki@gmail.com

VickiParkerRF@gmail.com

https://VickiParker.MyRandF.com

http://bit.ly/BankOnVicki

Connect with me at https://linktr.ee/Vicki%20Parker

# Amy Fritz

## *Now I Lay Me Down to Sleep*

On October 26, 2000, I heard those words that no one ever wants to hear, "You have cancer." What started out as a lump in my right breast, turned into my worst nightmare. I found a slight abnormality a couple of months earlier. However, I was reassured by my OBGYN that it was nothing to worry about. It could be a fibroid cyst, for instance. Breast cancer at my young age was unheard of back then. Regardless of her attempts to appease me, tears shot out of my eyes, while I sat there on the other end of the phone speechless. As a 25-year-old senior undergraduate at the University of Washington studying Atmospheric Sciences, I felt like my life had been moving forward in a positive direction. It was like a freight train charging along the track. Someone then suddenly pulled the emergency stop. My stomach jumped into my throat, while my heart pounded uncontrollably. I realized that this could kill me. Thousands of people die of cancer every day. I didn't want to die. I was much too young. I still had my whole life ahead of me.

I took a deep breath in, and let it out slowly. I let my mind finish racing, as I barely understood the medical jargon my doctor was using. I felt like I was Charlie Brown listening to his teacher and all I got was, "wawah wah wah Invasive Ductal Carcinoma wawah wah wah wah." If you are like I was back then and have never heard of it, it's a tumor in the milk duct of a breast that has spread beyond the duct. This is common form of breast cancer. However, it can grow and spread quickly. Therefore, early detection is important. I was fortunate that I found it early. Thank goodness I was taught to perform self-exams every month in my early teenage years. It was not in a mammogram or ultrasound. I found the lump!

In my second breath, I asked my doctor what our plan was. I like plans; to know what actions to take, is comforting to me. Our plan was to make sure I had clean margins around the biopsy (aka another surgery to make a slightly larger hole than what was left from the biopsy six days earlier), followed by radiation treatment. That sounded so simple! I was amazed. Was I really getting off this easy?

As a college student, I was hoping that we could pursue this path for treatment with as little interruption to my education as possible. After all, this was my last year and I was paying the bill. Tuition is not cheap. My team of doctors agreed that we could hold off until after I completed mid-terms in a few weeks. This gave me a chance to talk to my professors and also come up with a plan for my education. I was also working and needed to let my boss in on the news. Everyone was very supportive. They agreed that I could work and conduct my studies from home. This was revolutionary at the time. It was before online classes and telework.

We make plans, then life happens. For me, this was another tumor. Yes, I found another lump in the same breast diagnosed again as invasive ductal carcinoma. This was only a few weeks after the first diagnosis. What was happening to me? My doctors and I agreed it was time for a new plan and a more aggressive course of action. There would be no more waiting until after mid-terms. This was urgent. It was time to remove my breast and discuss chemotherapy, in addition to radiation treatment. Unfortunately, this would severely impact my education. My doctors urged me to take a break from college and work altogether. The treatment was going to take the rest of the school year into summer. I am not one to quit. I agreed to drop a few courses, but keep my favorite and hardest one, Dynamic Meteorology. I really liked the class, and my professor was very supportive. My boss also wanted to help out and gave me a research project that I could do at home. This would allow me to stay employed, without being in the office.

In November 2000, I had a modified radical mastectomy of the right breast and started a course of seven rounds of Cytoxan, Adriamycin and 5-Fluorouracil, aka 5-FU (CAF) which would be followed by 40 rounds of radiation. For those of us not in the medical world, this is some nasty stuff. The chemo could burn up my veins, so they put a Port-a-Cath in my chest to administer the drugs straight into my heart, the bodies best blender for mixing this medicine into my blood stream, without causing harm to my veins. The nurse who administered the 5-FU wore an exposure suit and thick gloves. Being diagnosed with cancer twice now, I needed strong medicine.

It was a tough battle. I lost my hair, my strength, my muscle tone and my energy, all in the first couple rounds of chemo. Then I lost a lot of weight and, worse of all, the ability to regain my immune system (white blood cell count) by the fourth round of chemo. I was just barely halfway through the journey and I looked awful. The doctors told me my body could not handle any more treatment, since my white blood cell count was not recovering, no matter what drugs they gave, which at the time was G-CSF. After several weeks of trying, I was not bouncing back.

I agreed with the doctors. I was exhausted. I could hardly climb a flight of stairs, without running out of breath. Just getting ready in the morning sapped me of most of my energy for the day. Then the doctors suggested that I get my affairs in order. That night I prayed a familiar prayer, "Now I lay me down to sleep. I pray the Lord my soul to keep. And if I die before I wake, I pray the Lord my soul to take."

I felt like I was living one of those Make-A-Wish foundation commercials. I needed more than a wish. I needed a miracle! So, I made a unique request. My favorite scriptures are, "A happy heart is good medicine and a joyful mind causes healing," Proverbs 17:22, and "the joy of the Lord is your strength" Nehemiah 8:10. These scriptures got me through tough times before, like when loved ones died. I needed them now more than ever. I needed to renew my strength and find my joy. I wanted to take a trip to the happiest place on

Earth. If this was it, I wanted to go out with a smile. Reluctantly, my doctors agreed. They knew this was very risky, because the slightest infection could quickly take me out. They equipped me with shots to support my immune system, face masks, gloves, hand sanitizer and lots of advice on how to avoid viruses and infections.

In mid-March 2001, barely able to walk through the airport, I boarded a flight to California. I went to Disneyland! I couldn't think of a happier place. The first day there, bald and weak, I was wheeled around the park in a chair. The staff gave me the VIP treatment and sent me to the front of every line. It took a lot to laugh that day, but I did! The next day I woke up with peach fuzz on top of my head feeling better and stronger. I was offered another wheelchair, but used it sparingly. The third day my hair was long enough that I no longer looked like I was fighting cancer, and no longer needed a wheelchair. The color in my skin was back, and a little tan from that wonderful California sunshine. By the fourth and last day in the park, you wouldn't have recognized me. I was running around, riding the rides, eating everything and giggling the whole day. I got my miracle. I was me again!

Upon returning home, I followed my doctors' orders and went in for a check-up. Their jaws dropped! They didn't recognize me. I had gained weight, strength, skin color and most importantly, HOPE. The Lord renewed my strength and now I knew I could do this. My blood work was back to normal and I could finish the three remaining rounds of chemotherapy. It wasn't just an outward change; it was on the inside too. I became unstoppable.

That spring changed my life forever. I knew I had what it takes to beat cancer. I finished chemo, and that summer I finished radiation too. The doctors continued to keep a close watch on me, but we knew the battle was won! The following spring, with a scholarship from the University of Washington Alumni Association, I graduated with honors. I also worked hard to rebuild my body and regain the strength that the drugs took from me. I hired a personal trainer and worked out with supportive friends. A year later, I completed the

Danskin Triathlon as a member of Team Survivor, placing in the top third of thousands of other female competitors.

During my battle with cancer, my doctors gave me lots of advice. Make sure you get enough sleep, eat plenty of protein (65 grams per day!), don't over exert yourself, stay home when your white blood cell count is low, avoid people with illnesses and be patient with yourself. One piece of advice they gave me, really resonated with me — make a plan for your future and focus on that, not on cancer. This reminded me of a scripture I learned when I was young, but didn't fully appreciate until now "Where there is no vision, the people perish," Proverbs 29:18. I started the battle with cancer in college, and I was not going to let the disease take that away from me. In fact, I wanted to one up it! My plan was to go to graduate school. That is what I focused on, when I was fighting! I had not finished radiation treatment, but I requested applications from prestigious universities all over the country.

In 2003, I attended graduate school at the Pennsylvania State University. While taking classes, I learned that the cancer was gone, but the battle was not over. Chemotherapy took its toll on my brain. I battled memory issues and struggled to retain what I learned, then recall during exams. I nearly flunked out my first semester. I was shocked! I recently graduated at the top of my class. I was now at the bottom. During my battle with cancer, I learned to ask for help. I saw a neurologist to learn how to strengthen my memory and retain knowledge again. Months of hard work paid off, and I was back on track earning A+ grades.

I still was not done, however. I also needed reconstructive surgery. Though I needed time to regain my strength and put on weight, insurance would not cover surgery if more than three years had passed after treatment. It was a tough now or never decision. I didn't have much time. I was nearing completion of my college work, but it would be too late if I waited till after I finished. I went for it, and defended my master's degree only a few weeks after another major surgery. With help of a neurologist, great surgeon and patient graduate advisor, I earned a Master's Degree in Meteorology in two years, finishing healthier and stronger than I started. Ironically, I still did not have my fill of graduate school. I went on to earn a second master's degree from North Carolina State University in Physical Oceanography.

In 2010, with two master's degrees under my belt, I was content with my education and ready for the next adventure. I moved to Maryland and started my career at the National Oceanic and Atmospheric Administration's (NOAA) National Weather Service (NWS) as a Meteorologist. Over the past ten years, I have enjoyed many opportunities to work on projects, like modeling storm surge from landfalling hurricanes to starting a mentoring program for early career professionals. Most recently, I have been the Program Manager for the National Weather Service's Cooperative Observer Program. This is a volunteer program that started in the 1890s, in which U.S. citizens from all over the Northern Hemisphere measure the daily maximum and minimum temperature and precipitation from which the U.S. climate record is written. I am honored to lead this highly dedicated group of 10,000+ volunteers.

Little did I know when I moved to Maryland, that I was about to start another adventure as well. My beloved cousin asked me to run a marathon with her near the Grand Tetons in the summer of 2011. While training for the marathon, I ran into a tall, dark, handsome man named Ryan Fritz on a trail. His bright smile drew me in like tractor beam in a sci-fi movie. I invited him over for a home-cooked meal, and have been cooking for him ever since. He was the best prize for running a marathon.

Dating was not easy. After all, being intimate with someone after having a mastectomy and reconstructive surgery brings on a whole new set of challenges. Most people I knew who fought breast cancer talked about looking forward to seeing their grandchildren again, not dating. There wasn't anyone in my life who could help me through the conversation of two boobs, one boob, old boob, new boob! Where was Dr. Seuss, when I needed him?! I was so nervous to tell Ryan, that it kept me up at night. In the end, it didn't matter at all. Ryan saw my inner beauty and was not at all deterred by my battle scars. We got married in May 2013.

Ryan Fritz also had a dream in his heart. It was to one day own his own business. He is a highly-educated world class personal trainer and certified strength and conditioning specialist (CSCS) with very unique skills. His plan was to start a company focusing on health and fitness. Well, he married the right person! Thriving in life after cancer, I am keen on a healthy lifestyle, that includes a well-balanced diet and exercise. Together, we started Science of Cardio (www.ScienceOfCardio.com). Our business focuses on coaching low impact sustainable work-outs both in-person and virtual, alternative non-conventional workout methods, setting goals, maintaining motivation and a healthy lifestyle. We enjoy setting a good example for our clients through our adventures together skiing, cycling, kayaking, hiking, surfing, swimming, running and much more. We hope to inspire others to make good decisions through our example of a healthy, thriving lifestyle. We have also developed tools for them, such as training videos, blogs and scientific podcasts, and offer personal training sessions, consultations and more. We focus on facts supported by current scientific research to offer the most efficient and effective wellness strategies. Our methods keep not only our clients healthy and happy, but me as well.

With the challenges I have faced, and victories I celebrate, I have learned many lessons. Three stand out that I will share. They are to make plans, laugh, and love.

**Make Plans**

Just as my doctors instructed me while I was fighting cancer, you should make plans for your life. This is particularly important, when you are going through difficulties. If you focus on the difficulty, you can easily get stopped there. Instead, see yourself through the difficulty. Imagine what you will look like celebrating the accomplishment of getting through it. I made plans to go to graduate school. That is not for everyone, but finishing your education might be. You must find something that excites you and lights a fire in you. You know you found it when thinking about it makes you smile, when you want to share it with others and when you count down the days until it comes to pass.

Taking a trip is a great plan. Most people enjoy traveling, even if it is a local adventure. When I finished graduate school, I wanted to go Europe, particularly the Eastern Mediterranean. I wanted to travel with someone who could be silly with me, not deterred by being in a foreign country, or the cost. Ryan was, and still is, my perfect traveling companion. We traveled to Europe in 2012, visiting friends in Germany. We then took a cruise with them out of Italy, visiting Sicily, Turkey, the Greek Isles and Greece. No surprises, the following year we got married in Hawaii and returned for our five-year wedding anniversary in 2018. Travel is not the only type of plan you can make. So is learning a foreign language, or playing an instrument, reading a book or writing one. I still make plans and have learned how to hang glide, surf, scuba dive and telemark ski. The key is, if you are going through a difficult time, it must be something worth fighting for!

## Laugh

Second, and equally important to making plans when going through difficult times, and always, is to laugh. They say laughter releases positive endorphins, which support your immune system. A good belly roll is also good exercise (without the cost of a gym membership). When I was fighting cancer, my doctors encouraged me to limit the amount of negativity I was exposed to. This shows up in watching the news, being around angry or pessimistic people, or just putting yourself in stressful situations that can be avoided. Instead, they encouraged me to watch comedies, read funny books or comic strips and surround myself with uplifting people.

The same is true today. It is important to keep up with current affairs, but don't spend your entire evening watching the news. Put something funny or inspirational on afterward. Listen to happy music. There are plenty of great artists, who can brighten a mood with their lyrics and tunes. Pets and children as also great at inspiring laughter. If you have them in your life, be sure to play with them often. They will help to keep you young. If you don't, consider adding them to your life. Visit a pet shelter, or hang out with friends AND their kids!

## Love

Finally, love. Love yourself, love your life, love your family, love others and love God. After all, I know He got me through cancer, and will help those who call on Him. Life is too short to live without love in every aspect of it, and very rewarding when it is returned to you. Before anyone can truly love you, however, you must be able to love yourself. Love is like a hug. Unless you are able to receive one, you cannot give one away. I was stuck after cancer to let an intimate partner love me. I was ashamed of my body. On the outside, I looked normal, but under my blouse was a chest full of scars. I could say that I was proud of them, but honestly, I wasn't. I was embarrassed by them. I felt somehow diminished in value, because of what the battle left behind.

Some people said that I brought cancer on myself. In their opinion, I was somehow being punished for something I did. I felt like Job in the Bible. I didn't do anything. I wasn't a troublemaker, or rebellious in my youth. Although they were not true, those awful words stuck with me for a long time. The scars were a reminder. Let me tell you, no one brings cancer on themselves! Not me and not anyone. We know certain choices, like smoking, make you more susceptible to cancer. However, cancer isn't punishment for bad behavior. God does not punish us with it, either. Don't let your life slip by believing those lies. When people ask me why I had cancer, I learned the best answer is, "I don't know. I don't need to know. I beat it anyways!"

I am blessed to be with Ryan. It wasn't easy, but I learned to see myself the way he sees me, and the way God sees me. I am beautiful, even with the scars. Ryan doesn't see them. He sees a vibrant, strong young woman with an athletic physique, beautiful smile and a passion for life. Those are honestly his words. It is important that we all see ourselves this way, and have people in our lives that remind us of who we really are. It is our inner beauty that matters most. In the words of Rihanna, "Shine bright like a diamond!"

The battle I fought with cancer didn't stop me from living. It was the catalyst for living the life I love. I am a stronger person, and closer to our Heavenly Father for it. I know that He renewed my strength those many years ago at Disneyland. He did not inflict me with cancer, but He gave me the strength to beat it. I give God the glory and use my story to bring hope to many people going through difficult times. I support people fighting cancer, and enjoy celebrating with them, when the battle is won.

**Amy Fritz**

Amy Fritz is a joyous and faith-filled wife, sister, daughter, aunt, niece, co-worker, friend and 20-year breast cancer survivor. She knows firsthand how much cancer can affect the lives of those diagnosed, and everyone around them. For Amy, cancer looked like the end. However, it was instead the beginning for who she became. Since her battle, she earned a Bachelor's of Science degree from the University of Washington, then earned two Masters' of Science degrees from Pennsylvania State University and North Carolina State University. After college, she began her career with the National Oceanic and Atmospheric Administration and is currently enjoying serving in the National Weather Service as the National Cooperative Observer Program Manager.

Together, Amy and her husband Ryan Fritz started the Science of Cardio. They are helping to improve the lives of those around them, by promoting healthy lifestyles through exercise and nutrition. As the CFO and Marketing

Director for Science of Cardio, Amy enjoys inspiring and motivating others, by leading by example through her and her husband's many adventures. They enjoy cycling, skiing, hiking, kayaking, running, swimming, traveling and exploring new places, and most importantly, bringing hope to others. Amy and Ryan have an infectious joy about them. They are on a mission to spread that joy, wherever they go.

Amy is incredibly grateful for her friends and family, who helped her win the battle against breast cancer, and for her devoted and loving husband. She is also grateful for her friends who encouraged her to write her story to inspire others and bring hope to those battling cancer. She gives God the glory for being able to share her testimony with you and others.

Amy Fritz
Science of Cardio
206-795-3898
Amy@ScienceofCardio.com
www.ScienceofCardio.com

# Danica Joan

## *An Unexpected Calling*

Here I am, standing at the second story window of my English Tudor home with moving boxes all around. I desperately wish that 'this' move will be the solution. Our house is in foreclosure and my husband is convinced that moving to Virginia is the answer to our persistent financial worries. When you are in a situation that feels like you have no control, it is easy to convince yourself that 'this' time will be different and ignore the nine times before.

Standing at that window wondering how life had gone very wrong, I felt alone. I did not have friends I felt safe to talk to, and my religious background trained me to 'never speak ill about your spouse to anyone.' However, I did have one trusted friend, who I now call my angel. He somehow knew the boys and I needed his help. He popped in to see how our moving was going and saw me peering out the window. He whispered to me, "you are in an abusive marriage and you need to get out! My wife and I will help you." I really did not see myself as abused, because I had successfully navigated my husband's temper without physical violence. I had also become skillful at navigating his cruel verbal attacks. There were several instances of abuse; physical, emotional and psychological that my sons and I were subjected to, but I could defuse any situation to restore harmony to the family. I did whatever I could to conceal the dysfunctional realities of impending financial disaster and isolation from my children; and of course, the first person I had to convince was myself.

I was raised in a family where fundamental Christian teachings kept me convinced that submission to my husband was godly and secured me a spot in Heaven. I do not know what caused me to accept my friend's invitation to escape, but I did. I was not completely hypnotized by the reality of my circumstances. In fact, I spent many nights dreaming and praying for a non-confrontational escape. I even calculated that since my husband was 22 years older than me, maybe God would take him off my hands.

With the help of my angel and family members, we got out. I thought for sure that a healthy and happy future was in store for us all. My plan was to finish my education, become a schoolteacher and co-parent equally. For the first time, I would oversee my own finances, always hoping that my husband would somehow stabilize his. By equally sharing the responsibility of the children, I felt that would eliminate the stress that I blamed for his controlling temper. However, life did not go as planned. Far from it, in fact.

It was not long before my husband began his assault. His first strategy was winning me back. For six months, child exchanges were calm and friendly. We shared the children equally with a tradeoff every Sunday evening. I was hopeful that this was a sign we would have a peaceful and loving co-parenting relationship.

Then, just before the court hearing was to happen that would make our 50/50 time-sharing arrangement official, the first gut punch was thrown. A knock at the door, not from my children arriving as I had expected, but from law enforcement serving me an injunction for protection and accusing me of abusing the children. My husband was asking for sole custody, based upon these allegations. The guttural blow was from reading statements in the filing from my sons validating his accusations. After the officer left, I lay in a fetal position on my bed, naked, feeling helpless and hopeless sobbing for hours, until I had no more tears. My goal of making our lives safe and stable had abruptly shifted out of my hands. I remember begging God that day to take me home.

By the end of the first year of this six-year battle, my husband was awarded primary custody. I was given four nights a month. As a person whose whole identity was wrapped up in being a mom above all else, this was the dark night of the soul for me. Life had taken a devastating turn and it kept getting worse.

At the end of every visit, my husband took the children to the police station to file their weekly abuse report against me. There were also innumerable calls made to the Child Abuse Hotline. When he realized that school personnel were mandated reporters, he coached the children to fabricate stories of abuse every time they went to school, so counselors and teachers were obligated to file reports based upon the children's stories. By this time, the children were fully enrolled in the narrative that mom was the evil person who destroyed their happy home.

**Managing Alienated Children Takes Strategy. It Goes Like This.**

1. While the children are filing out of dad's front door to get into my car for our visit, PRAY!

2. Pretend to be oblivious to their insults, as they enter the car. The key is to keep them safe, until we reach our destination.

3. NEVER, EVER bring up how horrible they were during the previous visit. Guilt trips will have the opposite effect.

4. Shower them with praise, mentioning something they might have experienced at school, so they are reminded that I am interested in their lives.

5. Get them as quickly as possible to the safe zone (grandparents' house). This will reduce their ability to effectively carry out sabotage, because unconditional love will derail the mission.

6. Savor the precious few hours of the weekend, when their minds are distracted and unguarded.

7. Be prepared for the re-escalation of hostile behavior, as the children realize that dad will arrive soon to pick them up.

My parents and I lovingly divided and conquered, by creating a fun environment. We usually had cousins around, and lots of activities to keep their minds off the mission of making their "evil" mom break. To this day, my children talk fondly of our weekends at their grandparents' house. That was their bright spot during those traumatic years.

**When Your Opponent Is Starting Forest Fires on Multiple Fronts, It Can Feel Overwhelming.**

I could not take the children to restaurants, afterschool, or summer activities without receiving a scowl from staff or school parents, because the moment my children were spotted, they connected me as the evil abusive mom they had heard so much about. Even neighbors were recruited in the battle. One of my neighbors just happened to attend the Catholic church, where my children went to school. She soon began spying on me and filed an injunction against me, because some neighborhood children had vandalized her car with feces. She was convinced it must have been me. Many of these neighbors ended up on court summons as witnesses.

After six long years, the court battle finally ended. I used to say, "time wounds all heels," because I never had a doubt that eventually people would see the truth, even my children. DCF (Florida's Department of Children and Families) eventually realized that hundreds of abuse reports with no findings against mom was suspicious. There were many moments when a judge, counselor, educator, or social worker involved in the case had the power to reduce our suffering but were not educated on recognizing the dynamics of parental alienation, so taking no action was their safest action.

We had an extensive psychological evaluation done, but by that time, it merely validated what the court already concluded. At the end, I was offered sole custody. However, I knew that healing would not be done by a court verdict. Therefore, I held to my original commitment. The only way for these children to heal, was for them to not be caught in the middle and forced to choose sides. They did not need to feel like one side won and they were the prize. Their healing would come based upon what I chose outside of court hearings. So, I chose for both of us to be equal. The custody battle finally ended, so the healing could begin.

## You May Be Asking Yourself What Gave Her Hope and Strength?

In 2001, I spent innumerable hours attending college online. This allowed me to also do research. I was desperate to learn why my children were so toxic and how I could solve it. While searching, the term "parental alienation" popped up on my internet results. I immediately ordered the book "Divorce Poison" by Dr. Richard Warshak and began learning as much as I possibly could about the topic. 20 years ago, it was challenging to find anything substantial, but I could not give up. These were my precious children who were the helpless victims. I had to fight for them.

I integrated my research into a college assignment, by creating a website that curated and connected resources for families. This pain would be given over to a purpose to help other parents, so they did not have to start from scratch as I did.

In 2004, I incorporated Kids Need Both, Inc. as a non-profit organization. I stayed in the shadows not seeking attention. I just wanted to give other targeted parents hope but was too afraid to speak out loud. I also dealt with fear because the relationship with my children was so fragile. If I made my activities too visible, my children would again reject me. However, I could not risk that. It was obvious that I still had much healing to do.

## A Second Marriage, a Second Chance? Not So Much.

It was not until I got into my second marriage, that I realized I keep attracting men who seemed unable to respect women. By 2009, my husband was having an affair and I shamed myself again. I feared that that my children would again experience another traumatic breakup and this time it was all my fault. I was in utter breakdown, thinking, "God! Haven't I been put through enough?!"

My dear friend Lillian, who was one of my unexpected angels, saw me struggling and supported me any way she could with her soothing voice and kind words. She was there from the beginning of my custody battles in 2001. She was always available to listen to me whine and complain about how my life was not working out and always compassionately offering suggestions. This time she asked me to join her for a Special Introduction of the Landmark Forum being held at a nearby hotel. I assumed it was one of those network marketing presentations, where some larger-than-life guy stands on a stage convincing you to join their team and that their products will transform your life with wealth and happiness. I did not care what it was, because I just needed to get away from my circumstances for a few hours.

When we arrived at the event, there were about 100 people in attendance. It seemed that Lillian knew many of them. The leader was on the stage and talked about the benefits of registering for this course. However, I was more focused on how strangely friendly the assisting staff was. I assumed that they were the closers, and couldn't really be so happy. I had no doubt they were recruiting people to join a home-based business of some sort, which I was not interested in. However, I decided to sign up for the course anyway to distract from my miserable existence.

I had no idea how my life would be altered by attending that course. It was on the third day of The Landmark Forum when my eyes were opened for the first time. I saw things in the background that were running my whole life. Up until that point, I was totally blind to them. I was the puppet being moved by a puppeteer, and completely unaware.

In that sleep-deprived, cram-packed three-day course, I discovered that I was the one who put all the meaning into my life. I realized that I was holding the keys to my freedom and did not know it. The predictable future, without this awakening, was that I would continue to chase an elusive future endlessly for the rest of my life. The distinctions I learned allowed me to see that sometime in my childhood I decided that I was not important, and the world did not care about me. When I was five and my mom was too busy to give me attention because she was cramming for her nursing degree, or when I started middle school and did not feel like I belonged or when I didn't get first place in whatever I was competing for, that was further evidence that I was not good enough.

I realized that I was the author of my story. I created the meaning behind everything that happened in my life. If I am the author, I can rewrite my story and give it a different meaning. Suddenly, in an instant, I found my power. I was finally free! After that moment, I felt like Adam Sandler in the movie "Click" who fast-forwarded through his life hoping to find true fulfillment, only to discover the true meaning of life was within himself all along.

## That Weekend Was Like Being Born Again… "I Was Blind, but Now I See."

When I returned home, I saw everything from a new perspective. My husband was still in the depths of a very destructive path of substance abuse and an affair. Nothing was different from the three previous days, but I was a new creature. I was no longer a victim and no longer interpreted my circumstances as a reflection of my value. My circumstances do not dictate my happiness. From that point on, I knew I had the power to create my own life, and I did!

In the months that followed, I attended other courses which Landmark offered and forged friendships with those committed to their own empowered transformation. This newly discovered courage led me to create my first big event for Kids Need Both, Inc. In 2012, I hosted my first educational conference. It was titled, "Parental Alienation: Educational Conference and Workshop for those Impacted by High Conflict Families." Participants and speakers flew in from all over North America and the Caribbean. It was also broadcast live over the internet, and TV and radio stations gladly promoted the event. To this day, I am blown away with what I accomplished, based purely on blind passion, or as some like to call it, "being unstoppable."

My most recent creation, and by far the biggest, was birthed by a global pandemic. At the beginning of 2020, I was working with our planning team to create a spring family advocacy conference. This conference was scheduled to take place at the end of April. Then just like the speculative path of hurricanes in Florida, we started getting whispers that there was a pandemic heading our way. My team members looked to me for guidance, while feeding me the ever-growing cases showing up in China. Countries were closing their borders and by mid-March, our communities were closing as well. As the virus made its way around the globe, it became clear that we had limited choices. Our team worked tirelessly to promote a conference that was just weeks away. Most of the planning was set and waiting to unfold.

Months before, we declared that this conference was standing for families restored globally, but if it did not happen, we would have failed. It then all became clear to me in the word "globally." I realized that it would be the pandemic that caused our voice to expand! We were going virtual. With five weeks to go, we reached out to our speakers, who were scheduled to fly in from across the US. We asked them instead to record their lectures. We quickly investigated online platforms to host the content. Our conference had to deliver everything we promised, including live panel discussions and the ability to interact with our speakers. As the team and I quickly adjusted our sails, we found more experts willing to contribute presentations to the conference, which doubled our number of speakers. The panel discussion tripled. Because we went virtual, we had 12 countries participating. It was now truly a global conference!

We accomplished our goals and far exceeded expectations with the success of the conference. However, my planning team continued to meet, because there was something lingering, like there was still more work to be done. We were clear that families are hungry for empowerment, and professionals were eager to provide it.

As the team brainstormed in discovery of what would be the next incarnation, I could see an educational social media platform arise before my eyes. We each contributed a word to our collective creation. Empathy, Trust, Honor, Integrity, Acceptance, Safety, Empowerment, Collaboration, Love, and

Education. Those words brought forth into existence the first global community that empowers families. It was a network of professionals collaborating to help retain the eternal unity of the family bond. In that moment, I felt the hand of God blessing this collective of heart-centered individuals. Out of the ashes of our heartbreak, we are transforming families.

## Why Do I Do What I Do?

It has been 20 years on this journey learning why I chose that bumpy road that led to my purpose. Even now, I have sudden unexpected moments of discovery. Just yesterday, I was interviewing a psychotherapist. As she was telling her story of being an alienated child who now helps adult children recover from parental alienation, I had a sudden moment of clarity. I realized for the first time that my life began as a pre-written script. The alienation did not begin with my first husband, it began at least two generations earlier. In the middle of the interview, I abruptly exclaimed, "Oh My God! It was my grandmother!" My mother was a child of parental alienation, but there was no word for it in the 1940s. No wonder! My mom was made fatherless by her own mother, who refused to allow her to communicate with him. She was not allowed her own voice. She and her siblings grew up in extreme poverty. Her father was replaced by a stepfather, who left her feeling vulnerable and unsafe. At the age of 18, she was the only sibling who had the courage to arrange a secret meeting with him, risking the consequences, if her mother found out. She ultimately ended up being locked out of the house and being taken in by a boyfriend's family. That traumatized girl became my mother.

It now made sense that to create a healthy future, the past must be cleaned up and restored. My life was not interrupted by a bad marriage. My marriage was the predictable by-product unintentionally created, because of a mother who was desperately in need of healing. The cycle would continue with my children, if I did not break it.

## So, How Do I Break That Cycle?

- **Forgive.** Cease the need to make anyone or anything wrong for what happened. Accept the gift that the lesson has given you. You should also remember to forgive yourself.

- **Fall in Love with You.** Give yourself permission to love YOU selfishly. Just because you have two arms, that does not mean you should give one away. Write a list of the qualities that you see in yourself. Ask others to add to this list and claim those qualities.

- **Own Your Circumstances.** The only way to have power over your circumstances is to stop resisting the circumstances and own it. To resist is as silly as resisting the pandemic. Resistance brings needless suffering.

- **Drop the Meaning.** There is a difference between "what happened" and the meaning you place upon it. Consider, for example, that your child breaks their arm. However, the meaning (or the story) you put to it is, "I'm a bad parent, because I allowed my child to get hurt." No. The fact is your child's bone is fractured. That is all. When you add meaning to things, it evokes an emotion that may be self-shaming. This does not serve you.

- **Live in the Now.** Own the past as something that gave you wisdom, but do not live there. Do not live in a "what if" future, based in fear, either. Consider that the past no longer exists, and the future has not been written. Therefore, the only place to live and experience life is in the present.

The next step in my journey is providing hope and mentorship to others. I work with parents who find themselves in the emotional sewage of divorce or custody battles. I get to show them the shortest way out. I love that! I do that through mediation, custody coaching and through the ever-expanding community of Kids Need Both, Inc. Maybe 20 years ago, I might have chosen a different path if I knew in advance what I would endure. I now choose the road I took. It led me to know myself as powerful and unstoppable in restoring families globally. For me, that is all there is.

## Danica Joan

With over 20 years of experience as an educator, Danica provides families with workable solutions to their custody conflicts. She is a Certified Family Mediator with the Florida Supreme Court, Guardian Ad Litem, the author for Florida's Family Stabilization Parent Education curriculum and a personal custody coach. Her inspiration came from real-world experience in an isolating and abusive marriage. Danica ended the marriage in hopes of establishing stability for her children and sought a peaceful co-parenting relationship with her husband. Deep in the trenches of a relentless custody battle lasting over five years, Danica endured arrest, relentless child abuse allegations, rejection from her children and being ostracized by her community. However, she never lost sight of what was at stake, which was the hope of a restored relationship with her children.

During the darkest times, she juggled multiple jobs, while attending college to become an elementary school teacher and adjunct professor. Meanwhile, she was fending off court hearings, managing her alienated children and defending a barrage of abuse investigations. To help others who found themselves in a similar situation, she founded the non-profit organization, Kids Need Both, Inc, with a mission of educating those impacted by high-conflict families.

Danica has devoted her life to providing families and professionals with education and resources that help them navigate the custody system with confidence. She currently hosts a weekly podcast called, Custody Matters Live, and continues to work with parents through custody coaching and speaking engagements. Kids Need Both, Inc continually pursues solution-based projects that restore families.Her team just launched an authoritative online community platform with family support resources, services, and live coaching from vetted experts with a likeminded vision of bringing healing to hurting families globally.

Danica Joan, M.Ed
Kids Need Both, Inc
P.O. Box 2022
Lakeland, FL 33806
863-420-5437
Danica@DanicaJoan.com
www.DanicaJoan.com

# Birgit Lueders

## *What in the world is "IRIDOLOGY"?*

I always loved reading, I thought to myself, as I carefully emptied boxes full of books, that I hadn't seen for a quite a long time. I was finally able to move to a quaint townhouse with a big library, after years of struggle to finalize my divorce. Every single book in my hand, reminded me of my years of discovery and search for wisdom. I didn't own a single fiction book, but hundreds of books about positive manifestation, Buddhism, Hinduism, Wayne Dyer, self-discovery, yoga, Bhagavad Gita, emotional freedom tapping, energy healing, Reiki, vibrational healing, light healing, herbalism…you get the picture. I have always been a seeker of knowledge.

It all started when I was young. After I finished school in Austria, I announced to my family that I was planning to go to America as a nanny. I wanted to know how it feels to speak English all day long and live in America. My Mom was immediately against it, but gladly my father gave me the green light to do so.

I still remember that I was 19 years old and in my hand I had a handwritten note with an address, when I arrived at the JFK Airport in New York. Remember that in 1992 there was no internet, and nobody had cell phones. After a long ride from the airport to Philadelphia, I finally arrived tired, hungry and nervous to meet the family who agreed to host me for a year as their nanny for their three little boys. Long story short, it was quite an adventure. I still believe that this experience has shaped me to get through any hardship in life. I did not understand the language, I had no family nor friends, I was homesick and hardly had any days off from work. I somehow still managed to make friends and enjoy my year of cultural differences.

Everything in life has a purpose and meaning. I believe that there are no coincidences in life. A few years later, I applied for a job at The American Express Bank in Vienna, Austria. As luck would have it, my boss happened to be from Philadelphia. He grew up in the same suburb where I was an au-pair. Coincidence? I don't think so. Life is like a tapestry and all our paths are already woven out. He hired me right away and groomed me towards an amazing career in the currency trade department. You could say I was heading towards a successful future and career in the finance world.

Unfortunately, I did not feel fulfilled. The business world is very dry. It is a dog eat dog world. Each day was like the movie "GROUNDHOG DAY. In case you have never seen this movie, it is about a guy, who wakes up every day and relives the same day over and over again. This is how I felt every single morning before I went to work.

One morning I was reading a newspaper and found a tiny ad on the bottom of the paper, which said "Flight Attendant Audition". The next few days were a blur. I ended up at that audition and made it through vigorous interviews in different languages. I even was weighed and measured! Yes, at that time flight attendants still had to be a certain height and weight.

A few days later, I quit a high paying job to become an Austrian Airlines flight attendant. For the next three years, I travelled all over the world. When I was not traveling to Japan, China, Australia, India, South Africa, and America as a flight attendant, I used my free flying privileges to travel even more.

During those years of traveling, I always had a keen interest in seeing how local people lived. What kind of food did they eat? What made them happy? How did they stay healthy? What kind of herbs did they use? I even visited their spiritual monuments to observe how they worshipped their "god(s)".

My interest about healthy living was deeply embedded in my DNA from many generations before. My grandmother at home in Austria introduced me at an early age to herbalism, showed me plants and explained to me how they can be used. She always had some mason jars with herbs at the windowsill. She was very spiritual and deeply religious. Her spiritual belief made her stay positive and thankful every day of her life, even during World War II.

Throughout my travels, I collected herbal lotions, elixirs, tinctures, crystals, spiritual stones, religious sculptures, etc. I was searching for something! During these times, I was convinced that I would find something unique and special, somewhere in the world. I just didn't yet know what it was.

Fast forward a few years and my carefree time came to an abrupt halt. One morning, my mom called me at my fiancée's apartment in Philadelphia and told me that my Dad had pancreatic cancer. I remember this moment very clearly, like it was yesterday. On that day, my fiancé and I were planning to look for an apartment, since our wedding was just a few months away. After my Mom's call, I was walking behind the realtor, and all I remembered were my mom's words "Dad has cancer".

During the following weeks, I stayed close to my Dad, visited him in the hospital and tried to stay as positive as possible in front of him. Unfortunately, my Dad died eight weeks after his cancer diagnosis, and two months before my wedding in Stone Harbor, NJ. I remember standing at the funeral, looking at my Dad's grave and hating everybody around me who still had their Dad. Up to this point, I truly had a picture-perfect childhood. You could say it was like the movie The Sound of Music. I never once thought I had to overcome a hardship like this, especially a few weeks before my wedding, and my permanent move to America.

Losing somebody that quickly, made me question everything about health and life itself. I was confused and upset about how my Dad could die so quickly, when he never showed any real symptoms. Yes, he had indigestion here and there. Yes, he had an extremely stressful job. However, was that enough of a reason to die from cancer? My Dad was 58 years old when he passed.

After my move to America, I was in a deep state of depression, culture shock and loneliness. I moved to a country where I did not know anyone. I just lost my Dad and I had to quit my job as a flight attendant because of my move. I had left everyone behind. Even a trip to the mailbox in Philadelphia confirmed my nonexistence. I did not even receive junk mail in my name. I was in a holding pattern of loneliness and darkness

This is when I threw myself into my holistic studies to find answers and to gain an understanding of how our body works. I needed to find out why my Dad had no symptoms and died with such little notice. Unfortunately, cancer is still a mystery to the medical and holistic world. The moment the medical establishment discovered my Dad's 10cm long tumor on his pancreas, it was already too late. To save his life, they cut out half of his digestive system, removed 2/3 of his pancreas, took out his gallbladder, cut out half of his small intestines and part of his stomach.

He never truly recovered from this procedure. After a month in the ICU, he was moved into a single room at the hospital and kept comfortable with high dosages of morphine, until he lost his battle with cancer. A few weeks before that, he walked by himself into the surgery room with a wave and a smile towards my mom! Who would have thought that he would never make it out alive? There must have been other options for him.

Maybe he could have lived several more years if he had chosen a more holistic natural path. One more year with my Dad would have made such a difference in my life. He could have walked me down the aisle during my wedding and seen me in my dress. He could have had one more dance with my mom, and one more kiss from each of his daughters.

Losing my Dad shaped me for the rest of my life. Because of it, I started my lifelong journey into the study of holistic healing, herbalism, energy healing, colorpuncture, holistic nutrition, yoga therapy and wellness coaching. One day, I finally found what I was looking for! After decades of searching all over the world for something special, I found IRIDOLOGY!

## What in the World is "EE-RUH-DAA-LUH-JEE"?

It turns out I have had several previous encounters with iridology during my travels. However, at this moment it all came together. Have you ever had a moment where something resonates with you on a very deep level? Let me take you to this moment.

I was finishing up one of the courses of my holistic nutritional class, when I found myself reading an article about iridology. Right there this author explained that IRIDOLOGY can evaluate the genetic strengths and weaknesses of the body systems, by assessing the iris color and fiber structures. As an example, he showed an iridology chart with a slight orange pigment in the pancreatic reflex energy zone. I ran to the mirror trying to see my own iris pattern and markings, almost blinded myself with a flashlight, and there it was, the same orange pigment. I am carrying a genetic weakness of my ancestors in the pancreatic zone. Wow!

You might think this revelation should have been worrisome for me! Does it mean that I might end up with pancreatic cancer, just like my Dad? No, it means that thousands of years ago, ancient healing masters knew a way to prevent disease, by noticing certain signs either through your eyes, your feet, your face and your tongue, before you showed any symptoms. For example, did you know, if you have fine lines on top of your upper lip, it can indicate weakness in your small intestines? Pulse, tongue, and facial assessment is nothing new in Chinese medicine or Ayurveda. It has been practiced for thousands of years.

Our body is a highly sophisticated machine. It makes sense that our eyes can reveal our genetic health through reflex responses from the rest of the body. Think about it. The first thing we notice about each other, is whether there is a sparkle in the eyes. It turns out that our eyes are not just the window to the soul, but also to the body.

The science-based iridology that I studied stems from the Europeans of the late 19th Century, which made it to America in the mid-1920s.

Unfortunately, iridology received bad publicity in the U.S. in the late 1980s, due to bad practices and inaccurate claims. However, all this changed after the International Iridology Practitioner Association (IIPA) was founded to create a high standard education in this field throughout the world, including the United States.

Why am I telling you this? Do you remember my years of trying to find myself? It all came to a close once I found this last piece of my so-called "life puzzle". After discovering iridology, I finally finished my education in the holistic field. I was now confident and proud to be a master herbalist, wellness coach and iridologist. I was ready to start my own business called BirgitCare. I finally knew what I wanted to do, which was helping others live a longer and healthier life. Just like Benjamin Franklin said, "An Ounce of Prevention is Worth a Pound of Cure".

Starting up a business in a field that is so misunderstood, demands focus, dedication and a healthy dose of fearlessness. I worried that nobody would take me seriously and that people might think I was another charlatan. Until to this point, I had some unpleasant encounters at holistic fairs, where people mad fun of me and bad mouthed me about what I was doing. One person even called me an eyeball reader, or a palm reader. It was very different for me, since where I am from, natural healing has always been part of our culture. Nobody ever questioned it or made fun of it. People actually understood its value, since it had been around for centuries.

I knew that starting a business in something people don't really understand, might be a rocky road. However, I was ready to overcome all of these obstacles, since I believed in what I was doing. I had a deep feeling that with my holistic therapies and assessments, I might be able to make a difference in somebody's life. I wanted to be there for people, who care more about preventive care than sick care.

First, I needed to get the word out about iridology! I started by becoming a regular speaker at several local health fairs, expos and holistic events. From there, I was able to receive invitations to bigger speaking engagements in places like Las Vegas, San Diego, Chicago, Boston, New York City and Australia. One day, I was very excited to receive a phone call from a TV show for my first television interview. I was ecstatic and freaked out at the same time. They called "ME" to come to one of their wellness shows to talk about iridology!

I had dreamed about this moment, but I honestly never thought in a million years that it would happen. I immediately agreed. I knew that I had to do this. However, suddenly my fears came alive. I felt panicked and scared. I had a great opportunity to promote my business. Reality set in, since I had never been in front of a camera. To call myself panicked, was an understatement.

I was at my first live TV interview almost hyperventilating and worried that I would make a fool out of myself. I had sweaty palms, dizziness, nervousness and anxiety. Once the interview started, it was all a blur. All I remembered afterwards was, that people from the live audience came up to me and asked me all sorts of questions about iridology. I was in a daze. Was I finally able to introduce and excite people about this old ancient form of assessment?

The TV interview aired several times throughout the upcoming week. However, I was not able to watch it right away, since I was worried that I came across as insecure and nervous. I was also concerned that my German accent might have been too thick, and the audience would have a hard time understanding me. A few weeks later, to my surprise, the host of the TV interview called me back for another chat on live TV about the emotional perspective of iridology.

After several years of steady clients, I finally let go of the fear that my business might fail. It takes time and patience to build a steady clientele within the first few years. Until people truly decide to come to an iridologist or an herbalist, they have pretty much exhausted all other resources. Many of my clients had gone through extensive medical and holistic treatments, without feeling any better. They ended up exhausted, disappointed and emotionally worn out at my office. However, they all had one thing in common. They became more open minded towards non- conventional therapies, since they had nothing to lose but a lot to gain.

My clients were willing to do whatever it took to get better. They listened to my suggestions and did not shy away from putting hard work and sweat into their efforts to heal their bodies. I am not a healer. I am a messenger of their body. I teach my clients to listen to their body. For a better understanding of how I am able to help my clients daily with iridology, let me tell you about one client.

Doreen (fictious name for privacy) had been struggling with symptoms, like heart palpitations, insomnia, weight gain and hair loss. She received the regular medical checkups for thyroid, EKG, hormones and blood tests. The good news was all her tests came back normal. However, the bad news was that she still did not feel any better. At this point, she was relieved, since she knew that she didn't have anything serious, like cancer etc. However, over the following months, she lost more hair and gained more weight, despite her very restricted calorie intake. She constantly felt tired due to her insomnia, which made it even harder to keep a positive and happy outlook on life.

She spiraled into depression and felt like she is losing control over her mind and body. This was especially true since nobody had a satisfactory answer to all of her symptoms. When she finally came to my office, I took a picture of her eyes. She had those typical circular looking loops called lacunae in her iris on top of her thyroid reflex area. When I asked her about her genetic background with thyroid issues, she confirmed that her mother had been on thyroid medication for a long time.

Doreen was my typical client. She was too healthy to pass any medical tests for hypothyroid, but sick enough to not feel well. Throughout the following three months, I supported Doreen's thyroid through herbal supplements. I also taught her how to eat a thyroid friendly diet. A thyroid friendly diet is a diet high in nutrients, minerals, vitamins and antioxidants. This diet was easily digestible and absorbable for her digestive system. Once her body started to absorb more nutrients, especially natural iodine, she started to feel better.

Her long-term strict calorie intake caused nutritional deficiencies. This affected her genetically weakest organ system, which was her thyroid. After a few months of using food as her medicine, and herbs like Irish moss, seaweed, black walnut and lemon balm, she was able to sleep better, lose weight and experience new hair growth. As you can see, she was incredibly happy with her results. However, for a permanent holistic approach, I needed to address all three parts of her body, including the physical, emotional and spiritual. Now that I was able to support her physical well-being, I needed to get deeper into her emotional healing. During an emotional iridology evaluation, I was looking into the association of emotions with specific organ systems. For example, lungs are affected by the emotion of grief. Stomach issues can be associated with excess worry. In Doreen's case, the thyroid was associated with speech or speaking from your heart. To enhance her spiritual and emotional energy in her throat, I had her work on speaking up, or even singing in her shower. She had always been very quiet, even as a child. She learned early on, that it was better to be seen than heard. Falsely speaking up as a child, could have ended in a whooping. Due to this upbringing, she was afraid of expressing herself, even if she was treated unfairly. As you can see, any physical symptom has its original source within an emotional experience. Everything is interconnected.

As I am writing this, I am wondering why my Dad died from pancreatic cancer. I now know that pancreas weakness is associated with the desire to find sweetness in life. My dad was born at the end of World War II and money was very scarce. Since he was the oldest of five children, he started to provide financially for his family at the early age of 14. He has been a hard worker his entire life. He was able to get a higher education, by working during the day as a carpenter and taking classes at night. When I was young, I was proud that my Dad was so indispensable for the company he worked for. He couldn't even go on vacation, without having long hours of business calls. However, with the knowledge I have now, I know he never even had a carefree, playful childhood. He was forced to grow up much too early.

I encourage all my clients that it is never too late to change the course of their life. Any physical pain they might experience, might just be a warning from the soul that they are on the wrong path. They may have come so far off from experiencing true happiness, that they needed to reevaluate and take a snapshot of their current life to find out where they have lost themselves.

During the time that my Dad was sick, I promised him I would live my life to its fullest. Life is short and a true gift from the heavens. Do not waste this gift, by accepting a mediocre life. Never procrastinate and wait for the time to come that you can do what you would love to do. There is never a better time than now. Nobody likes to get criticized, judged and made fun of. However, if you believe strongly in what you are doing, at the end the universe will pay you back tenfold.

P.S. Thank you, Dad, for telling me that I can do anything I want, as long as I believe in myself. I'll promise you that each day I will smile, laugh, and appreciate something. I will keep your legacy of positiveness alive.

## Birgit Lueders

Birgit Lueders is the mother of two wonderful daughters, Emma and Lisa, living in Philadelphia, PA. She is a certified master herbalist, yoga teacher, iridology instructor, and wellness coach. Birgit first learned the values of an organic herbal lifestyle in her home country of Austria. Since 2009, she has operated BirgitCare — a business focusing on health, wellness, and natural healing in Philadelphia, PA. Through BirgitCare, she offers personalized wellness coaching to support her client's emotional, physical, and spiritual well-being, by using modalities like iridology, herbalism, nutrition and Colorpuncture. In 2012, Birgit founded the Center for Iridology, where she is teaching iridology courses around the world and annually in major cities, like New York, San Francisco, Chicago, Boston, and Philadelphia. In 2020, during the pandemic, she adapted her iridology courses for online certifications and was able to move her wellness coaching program online. Throughout the past

10 years, Birgit has been a known speaker in her field at numerous national and international EXPO's, while being consistently featured on radio and TV. After being a Fellow, a Diplomat, and the Vice-President of the International Iridology Practitioner Association (IIPA), in 2020 Birgit became President of IIPA through 2023.

Birgit Lueders
BirgitCare, Center for Iridology
720 Whitetail Circle
King Of Prussia, PA 19406
484-844-5710
BirgitLueders@gmail.com
www.BirgitCare.com
www.CenterforIridology.com

# Lisa Edwards

## *Worthless Victim to Worthy Victor*

"I have a brain tumor".

Who'd have thought that those fateful five words would thrust me onto an unimaginable journey which would lead me, a mediocre nobody, to sharing my message globally through public speaking and on high profile podcasts?!

I know what you're thinking. It's going to be a story about illness, how I was almost at death's door and how I overcame a brain tumor, right? Well, not quite. In fact, not at all. My story is about a shocking betrayal and how I navigated my way through that, to uncovering an important hidden truth that would completely change the entire trajectory of my life.

So, where do I begin? OK, I'll start at the beginning. Sounds like a sensible starting point, doesn't it?

I met my partner through online dating. It was a baptism of fire into this bizarre virtual world, being old enough to remember the good old days, when people used to meet by locking eyes across a crowded room. "It'll be a great way to build up your confidence again," my best friend encouraged. Somehow, she managed to convince me.

Our first date was in Covent Garden in London. I nervously emerged from the tube station to the chorus of tooting horns from the passing red buses. Amid the chaos of rush hour, he was waiting for me, casually leaning against the railings, without a care in the world. He was slimmer, more effeminate and with longer hair than his photos. He had sad brown eyes that drooped downwards in the corners, reminding me of a St Bernard dog. I won't lie and say it was love at first sight. If anything, I was a little disappointed, but that seemed to be the story of my life.

I'd never been too successful in relationships. As a fiercely independent introvert, I found them awkward and suffocating. I tended to attract good men who fell in love with me quickly, and try as I might, the feeling was never reciprocated. I made a lot of mistakes and sadly, I hurt people. I'd labeled myself as damaged and abnormal because until my son was born, I'd felt incapable of feeling love. Over a year had passed since I'd left my son's father. We'd been together for almost nine years, the longest relationship I'd ever had. He was a good man and loved us but the feeling wasn't mutual and I was deeply unhappy. I stuck at it because I wanted my son to grow up in a stable home with two loving parents, something that I had not had. I repeatedly told myself that I should be grateful that he would never hurt me and to stop being selfish for wanting my own happiness.

You see, my childhood was full of trauma. The atmosphere at home was as dark and heavy as the ugly brown velvet curtains that used to hang at the living room window. My father was a heavy drinker who was violent towards my mother. She divorced him when I was eight and married another man who, at the time, was controlling and abusive, not only to my mother but also to me. I was hit, whipped and thrown down the stairs, among many other things. I could write several books on my childhood alone but I'm not going to go into detail here. As I'm sure you can imagine, I grew up with a dim view of men. I vowed that I would never allow any man to treat me badly like my mother had done, especially after I came home once to find her lying in a pitiful heap on the floor. She was upset because her abusive husband had left her. No man was going to reduce me to that, I thought.

The initial awkward date turned into a relationship. At this point, I should give "him" a name. Let's call him Peter. Peter had an unassuming personality that matched his St Bernard looks. He was laid back, affectionate, and eager to please. He hated arguments and never said a bad word to me. My son liked him and so did my family and friends. He grew on me and for the first time in my life, I let someone in emotionally. I accepted love and I gave it back. Now, don't get me wrong, it wasn't a deep, strong, passionate love but it was certainly more than I'd ever felt before. We did the usual things, spent our holidays abroad every year and had parties with my family. However, we didn't have much to do with his family. We had our ups and downs but it was mostly fine until the summer of 2014. That's when things started to unravel.

He came home late one evening, yet again. He was often late due to work commitments. This time I was pissed off and stressed. For a couple of weeks, on an almost daily basis, I'd been receiving abusive and explicit messages via Facebook and text from a female colleague who Peter worked with. I'd been unable to get hold of him on his phone one day. I made the mistake of sending her a message and asking if she could get him to call me. This seemed to be a green light for her to begin trolling me for some inexplicable reason. I'd never met her but from her Facebook profile, she was a gorgeous young blonde who, according to Peter, dressed quite provocatively at work. She claimed that I was too old, ugly, and bad in bed for Peter, and apparently, she could do a better job of satisfying him. She delighted in telling me how she was going to do that in great sordid detail.

As I began yelling at him - because, despite him assuring me his employer was dealing with it, it was still going on - he suddenly sat down in the chair and put his head in his hands. He said he'd just come from the hospital. "I have a brain tumor". I was stunned into silence and despite the summer heat, I suddenly felt ice cold. What do you say, when your loving partner drops that bombshell?

Over the coming days and weeks, Peter's behavior became more and more erratic. He insisted on going to work but would disappear for days at a time and switch off his phone.

He came back one night in a strange mood. He seemed agitated. He was drinking, even though I warned he shouldn't be. Feeling annoyed because he hadn't given me any coherent explanation for his disappearance, I went upstairs to have a bath. At one point, he barged into the bathroom and then plunged his hands down into the water and grabbed me hard between my legs. It was aggressive. When I got out of the bath and walked into the bedroom, he was standing there, naked, with a strange expression on his face. He grabbed me by the shoulders and began wrestling me down onto the bed. I kept telling him to stop and fought as much as I could. He was laughing at first and I thought he was joking, but he didn't stop. He was hurting me. He wasn't a big man but he was still stronger than me. This was not the Peter I had known for the last six years. I wanted to punch his face when he was on top of me but I was too scared to hurt him because of the brain tumor. What if I killed him? I scratched his arms so badly, that he had to wear long sleeves for weeks after, which I even felt guilty about! Afterward, I couldn't believe what had happened. I was shocked, confused and so upset I threw him out, although I believed it must have been because of the brain tumor. Maybe it was affecting his cognitive functioning? Maybe it was the stress and fear of dying? I had to find some way to explain it. He loved me, didn't he?

Sure enough, he came back a day later pleading with me to help him, as he was scared of dying. He said he had no one else and didn't want to worry his family. So, of course, I took him back in. I agreed to support him, as long as I was at every hospital appointment. However, I never made it to a single one because he kept changing or forgetting the times. I was becoming increasingly anxious and frustrated about it all.

One afternoon I began searching through his things for an appointment letter. I've never been inclined to go through anyone's stuff before, or since, but I couldn't ignore the gnawing feeling in my gut any longer. I didn't find any letter but I did find an old phone. It was mine. One that I had lost years earlier. What the hell was he doing with it? Why had he not mentioned it? As these questions were going through my mind, I could hear my heart pounding in my ears. There I was, standing in the bedroom with this small white phone in the palm of my trembling hand, holding it with as much fear and trepidation, as if it were a hand-grenade. Deep breath…here goes…

The first message I saw read "Do you want to come and meet your daughter or do you want to do a DNA test?" with a photo of a baby. Wow! I felt sick! If only that had been the worst of it!

Over the coming days, I found out more about my partner than I had known in six years. Each lie I uncovered felt like another Jenga piece being violently ripped from everything I had believed about my relationship until, rather cruelly, my whole world crashed down around me. He was also married! He had lied about his place of work. The female "colleague" who had been trolling me was fake! It was him who'd been sending me those messages! He had set up numerous fake Facebook accounts of "colleagues" to convince me of his lies. He had even lied about having a brain tumor!

What kind of person does that? And why? HOW COULD I HAVE NOT KNOWN? How could I trust anything or anyone anymore? And worse, still, how could I trust my judgment again? I felt like I was spinning deep underwater, disoriented, and unable to find the surface.

I'd truly believed I'd been in a relationship with a good person. Suddenly, I couldn't leave my house without feeling the stares and snickers behind me. If you have ever experienced humiliation in your life, either as a child or an adult, and you cast your mind back to that moment right now, then you'll probably still feel the excruciating pain as if it had happened yesterday, right? Interestingly, two Dutch psychologists, Otten and Jonas, conducted a series of experiments in 2013 which measured the brain activity of those feeling humiliation. Unsurprisingly, they found that it was a significantly more intense emotional experience than even anger, happiness or shame.

Consequently, I didn't seek help and I didn't talk about it.

I listened to motivating music and exercised obsessively. I booked a trip to do the four-day Inca Trek to Machu Picchu, which had been on my bucket list for about ten years. All that saved me from going too far down into the abyss. Was I OK? Well, I wasn't going to let "lying brain tumor man" beat me, now was I! I got right back on the horse. A little too quickly, I might add.

That "horse" turned out to be an incredible guy. He was funny, understanding, and gorgeous. The chemistry between us was electric. I would often find myself staring at him and wondering what on earth he was doing with me. He knew a bit about my previous relationship and he did as much as he could to alleviate my fears and trust issues, such as sending me his location on Google or photos of wherever he was. Despite his efforts, I couldn't let him in. We only saw each other when my son was with his father and I refused to introduce him to friends and family. After 15 months together, he did the kindest thing for me that no man had ever done before. He dumped me! You see, I wasn't OK. I mean, I didn't go as far as standing in the dark, repeatedly switching the lights on and off, or boiling his pet rabbit, but I didn't exactly make it easy for him. I went into that relationship with the mindset of a helpless victim, expecting him to fix me without taking any personal responsibility for my healing or behavior. The day we split was so painful. He was holding me tightly for such a long time, not wanting to let me go. It felt like my heart was being ripped in two. I crawled into bed that night, curled myself into a ball like a small child, and cried myself to sleep. It was my fault. I had messed up AGAIN. I couldn't even make it work with an amazing guy who I really liked! I was a 42-year old failure, destined to be alone.

Despite not wanting it to end, deep down I knew it was the right decision and so I accepted it. Even though I wasn't consciously aware of it at the time, he taught me a huge lesson about self-love, self-respect, and boundaries. I knew that he had strong feelings for me and ending it was just as painful for him. To recognize that his boundaries had been crossed and to walk away for his mental well-being took strength, courage, and deep self-worth.

There was no anger. I felt overwhelming sadness and self-pity. I stopped exercising, listening to music, and setting goals. I sank into a depression that turned into a physical illness. I lost weight, was in constant pain, and had no energy. After several months, it got so bad that I ended up in the hospital. I had convinced myself that I must have cancer. Instead, the consultant said there was no physiological cause for my illness and that it was most likely caused by stress. I was discharged.

Just knowing that there was nothing wrong with me, was enough for the symptoms to slowly begin dissipating. Incredible isn't it? The power of your mind and your beliefs!

It felt like a second chance. I knew I needed to change but, if I'm honest, my motivation was my son. I didn't want to gift him all my issues, which were seemingly more than the National Geographic. I decided that I wanted practical advice on how to improve my communication skills because I thought that was my main problem. I wasn't looking at the root cause, just the symptoms.

As luck, or synchronicity, would have it, there was an intensive NLP course going on locally, on the exact dates that my son was going away with his father. It just felt so right.

One of the most important things I learned in that course was Cause and Effect. Our knowledgeable (and very funny) trainer, who'd been trained by the co-founder of NLP, John Grinder, asked us on the first day "Are you on the Cause side, or, the Effect side?" While we cannot control what happens to us, we can control how we deal with it and move forward. I had spent my entire life on the Effect side and it felt liberating knowing that I didn't need to stay a victim, if I didn't want to. I could move over to the Cause side and start taking control of my life. It was a choice. Yes! He was talking to me and for the first time in my life, I was listening.

The training was intense. As I began peeling away the layers of my issues, a huge light was shone on my lack of self-confidence. It's ironic because on paper it looked as though I had a lot of confidence. I'd always been determined and seemed to have a natural ability to achieve anything I set my mind to. At the age of 19, I went to live in Italy with a one-way ticket and no money to return, finding jobs and making a life for myself. I also worked as a croupier, while traveling. I'd even completed a super scary skydive from 13,000 feet. Yet, this lack of confidence had followed me everywhere. I could never shake the feeling that everyone else was in some way better than me.

A few months later, I embarked on my next 150 hours of training. What I was about to discover this time, was going to completely transform my life.

It was the end of the course and we spent the day practicing breakthrough coaching sessions on each other. We were sat in the café of the hotel, an odd choice for a coaching session, I agree, but there were no more private spaces available. Our trainer came and joined us to silently observe, as I was "being the client". He listened for a while, as I was answering the thought-provoking questions that my colleague was asking. He then sat down next to me, slowly reached into his pocket, pulled out a packet of tissues, and placed them carefully on the table in front of me. I'll never forget the smell of fresh coffee wafting through the air, as he turned to me and in a low voice said "Forgive me Lisa, but why do you hate yourself so much?" Ouch! It stung like a slap in the face! I just burst into tears. I didn't care that there were people around. I cried for all the years I'd held this pain inside of me.

I could suddenly see with the pristine clarity of the freshly washed glasses, that I could hear being emptied from the steaming dishwasher behind me. While I'd been projecting all the bitterness and blame outwards towards my parents, my ex, and anyone else who'd ever wronged me, it was, in fact, myself that I hated. I'd either attracted negativity into my life or unconsciously sabotaged the good, simply because I had felt unworthy and undeserving. This was the reason why my entire adult life had felt like I'd been trying to fly a kite without any wind. It had been one continuous cycle of running hard and fast to get my kite up in the air. If I was successful, it was only ever for a fleeting moment before it came crashing back down and I began the whole exhausting process again.

Using a powerful combination of modalities, such as self-hypnosis, NLP, and affirmations, I rewrote the script of my internal dialogue. I learned to love myself unconditionally, to be OK with my imperfections, and to see that my failures were just learnings. I started to take ownership of my thoughts and emotions, to forgive myself for past mistakes, and to forgive everyone else. Forgiving those who'd wronged me was not for them, it was for me. I wanted to own my story and NOT allow my story to own me anymore. The last remaining shackle of victimhood was removed. Above all, I began to believe that I am worthy, I am deserving, I am good enough, and that I have all the resources within me to be completely UNSTOPPABLE, just like I know you have too, haven't you?

Since learning self-love, my kite is soaring high with far less effort. I now have my own coaching business helping other women achieve complete self-belief and inner confidence, so they too can create the life they deserve. For the first time in my life, I'm in a truly happy relationship. I got back together with the amazing guy of my story three years ago and we are stronger than ever. Last year I did something I never imagined I could ever do – in fact, it used to be my worst nightmare! I gave a public speech in London in front of doctors, entrepreneurs, and the seven-figure media mogul and London Real founder, Brian Rose. It was also streamed to thousands of people globally on social media and the feedback I received was mind-blowing. Since then, I've been featured on many podcasts and have been approached by a TEDx organizer. Hopefully, once this pandemic is over, I will get to stand on that red spot.

I'm not going to tell you that true success and happiness are not found outside of yourself but within you. Nor am I going to tell you that they come from aligning with your values and knowing your worth. I'm not going to tell you that real success comes when you have unshakeable self-belief because you know you deserve it, either. As I know you will find all this out for yourself, when you embark on your own journey to self-love, won't you?

Take a moment, right now, to imagine how incredible your life will be, when you fully realize just how worthy and deserving you are...see what you can see...hear what you can hear...feel what you can feel...

Ah, isn't it wonderful?

**Lisa Edwards**

Lisa Edwards is a certified and accredited Master Practitioner of Hypnotherapy, Time Line Therapy™ and NLP. She has also recently trained in the wonderfully therapeutic Havening Techniques® and is looking forward to weaving that into her work in the near future. She is a motivational speaker and regular podcast guest, sharing her message, knowledge, and expertise.

Lisa has had a far from mediocre life, although she always felt mediocre and unconfident as a person. From a young age she knew that she wanted to travel and to be as far away from her oppressive childhood as she could. She spent most of her adult years living a nomadic lifestyle, moving from place to place and country to country, trying her hand at everything from teaching English to dealing roulette. Lisa has always had a natural gift for manifesting everything she focused on, long before she had even heard of The Law of

Attraction. Despite her ability to achieve her goals, it was the longevity of success and happiness that always eluded her. A trauma in adulthood put her on the path to self-love with the realization that the fundamental key to true success and happiness is believing that you are worthy of it.

Lisa's philosophy in life is to live it in the same way we are encouraged to eat a nutritious balanced diet – with as much color and variety as possible! She has run two half marathons, raised money for charity by skydiving, trekked the four-day Inca Trail to Machu Picchu, and ridden a toboggan down from the Great Wall of China. Lisa lives in the UK. She is a proud mother to an awesome son and has a wonderful partner.

Lisa Edwards
Hypnotherapist * Speaker * Coach
International House, 12 Constance Street
London, E16 2DQ, UK
Admin@LisaCTEdwards.com
www.LisaCTEdwards.com

# Laura Fank-Carrara

## *Here's Me*

Ever since I was a little girl, the only consistent dream I would lie awake at night thinking about was one day having kids and becoming a mom. I'd picture tons of perfect babies, the perfect husband and the perfect little house with a giant white picket fence wrapped around the entire thing. To me, having that fence would represent serenity, a happy home and a fulfilled life. People with white picket fences always seemed to be living the happiest lives. That's what the movies portrayed, anyway. While having that dream heavy on my heart, I managed to 'blink', and before I knew it, I was living in a beautiful home with my husband and five amazing babies. We really did it have it all — the white picket fence included.

Those babies quickly became my 'why' and my motivation for everything that I did. It was a dream come true to be a stay at home mom and wake up every single day to care for them and experience each of their bold personalities come to life. All I wanted to concentrate on was these incredibly smart, hilarious and perfect humans. As you can imagine, juggling five of them all under the age of six was a major job in itself. I really didn't seem to have time to do anything else, nor did I want to.

Since my attention was focused on them for such a long time, it was hard for me to really notice that my marriage started to fall apart. I guess I expected the marriage to just work without the actual work. I mean, how could it not? We had the white picket fence!

I managed to 'blink' again. Before I knew it, I was no longer just a mother of five. I was a *single* mother of five. This was not how my story was supposed to go and I never imagined that it could actually happen to me. Our ten-year marriage ended with so much resentment, anger and hatred, that it left me and my kids financially strapped and struggling.

One morning in 2004, I woke up just before sunrise to begin the day. The coffee was brewing and I remember starting to hear little giggles come out of the kid's rooms, as they also began to slowly wake up. As I was getting the house ready for another day, I opened up the living room blinds to find that my car was missing from the driveway. I frantically called the police and was notified that my vehicle had been repossessed.

Our chain of events just never seemed to get any better. We were always financially struggling and unfortunately, others really began to notice. Later that year, our church awarded my family with a free Thanksgiving dinner. As nice of a gesture as that was, I couldn't help but feel ashamed, embarrassed and completely helpless. I wanted very badly to believe that another family needed that dinner more than we did. However, I knew at the bottom of my heart that I would not have been able to provide that holiday meal for my kids, if it wasn't for our church.

As a young mom, I didn't realize how often there would be times that I would need to navigate outside of my safe haven. When more stressful situations would occur, I had no brain power left to think or deal with it. I had no direction. Where was my life GPS, when I needed it? Through all of the negative events that always seemed to be happening at that time, I started to lose my sense of worth. Even though I was losing who I was, I always seemed to find a little bit of it, when I looked at the little faces absorbing my every move. My place in this world was with them and that was all I really ever needed. They were and still are my white picket fence.

**Trapped and Strapped**

Being a single mom, there were many challenges that I had to navigate in order to give my kids the life they deserved. Just how I was going to do it was the challenge. Thankfully, I did not have to navigate alone. Towards the middle of my marriage, we decided to add an in-law arrangement onto our single-family home. Being a family girl through and through, I did not hesitate to have my mom and sister move in, when my mom started to undergo some health issues. Having them there was a blessing that I will never be able to repay. However, it still didn't completely take away the challenges of being a single mom of five. How was I going to work? I couldn't put that burden on my sick mom to take care of my kids every single day. Where could I get someone to watch five kids and still make enough to pay the bills? These were all problems I faced on a daily basis, that I continued to search for the solutions to.

I knew I needed to make some serious changes. I knew I needed to put on my big girl pants and get my warrior, single "mama mentality" in check. Deep down I knew that I was so much stronger than this. I just had to keep reminding myself of my 'why.' From there, I began to take classes, immersed myself into self-help programs and searched for jobs that would be flexible enough to work with our lives. I ended up with a few odd and end jobs that worked around my schedule. I took on projects that I was able to do from home and then bartended at night. I was truly blessed to have crossed paths with some amazing people and employers that offered support and flexibility for me.

**Happily Ever After 2.0?**

They say when you least expect it, someone will come along and make you realize why it never worked out with anyone else. During that low point in my life, I met a man that redefined the meaning of love for me. I could not believe someone was actually accepting me for me and also loved my five young kids enough to help take care of us all. He took charge, took all of the burdens off of me and provided the peace and contentment that I was so desperately seeking. I loved every minute of him taking the wheel. However, I didn't realize that I was beginning to depend on him for everything and I was giving up on myself in the process. He did crave control and at the time, I did not see this as a problem. I just loved having him there and I saw it as him wanting to take care of us.

We went on to date for thirteen years. During those thirteen years, we had discussed marriage many times. However, something in my gut was not letting me follow through. Because I "loved" him more than I loved myself, I gave up my health, some of my relationships and the wheel to my life, just to please him and keep him happy. To the world, I was the happiest woman to ever exist. However, when I was alone and staring at myself in the mirror, I could not recognize the woman that was staring back at me.

I was emotionally beaten to my core and didn't know how to navigate my way without him. That is why I stuck it out for thirteen emotionally taxing years. I knew I was accepting unforgivable behaviors: cheating, consistent emotional abuse, threats, etc. I just thought I wasn't strong enough to fight the heartache that would only intensify, if I left. During all those years, I continued to choose what I thought was the lesser of the two evils. I closed my eyes and kept my head in the sand, just to not feel or deal with the hurt publicly. It was torture to keep the happy face on for my kids when in reality, my heart was in a million pieces. I knew I needed to face and work through these vulnerabilities to prepare for the inevitable that was soon coming.

I mustered up the little bit of self-respect I had left and began extensive counseling. I also decided to work a little more, take fitness classes and eat better. I began to go to church regularly and poured all my attention into God, my kids and work. It was time to show my kids and myself the definition of resilience.

**Redefining Me**

It was time to take matters into my own hands. Instead of seeking validation outside of myself, I began to seek inward. What type of woman and mom do I want to be? If I wanted to be a strong, unstoppable and resilient woman, I needed to start taking the hard actions that showed that. I was determined to have the mindset that from here on out, every negative thing that was inevitable to happen would just be a part of my story. I refused to stand by and let them define me.

In 2015, I was diagnosed with a bicuspid valve in my heart which, in turn, caused an aortic aneurysm. At the time, I thought my doctor had just handed me my death sentence. After finding out that this diagnosis is hereditary, I frantically had all of my kids tested. Thankfully, no one else had been affected. It was a long and scary process and something I had to adapt to. With this new information, I took the steps to tap back into my "mama mentality" and decided that it was not going to define me. This is just another small part of who I am and something I will take the steps to control for the rest of my life.

Later that same year, I lost my dad unexpectedly in his sleep. He lived across the street from us and was a part of our everyday lives. He was the only consistent father figure that my kids ever had and the most selfless, family man there ever was. By that point, I had dealt with many heartbreaks. However, this was by far the most horrific heartbreak I have ever endured. I spiraled into a depression so deep, that I needed medication to help me function. My kids also took it incredibly hard. Not having him around was another huge obstacle that we all had to face together.

I couldn't seem to dodge this chain of negative events. My ambitions and goals seemed very easy to achieve one day, yet so impossible the next. I kept reminding myself that these events had to be happening FOR me and not TO me. I no longer wanted to play the victim. but it was very hard to think positively during such a difficult time. I knew that if I wanted to do anything with my life, I was going to have to fight.

I was fortunate enough to land a few pretty good jobs along the way that helped to pay the bills. After getting a great full-time job at Redfin, I went back to school and got my real estate license. I later went back and got two more state's licenses. Getting those licenses was just as physically draining as it was mentally difficult. This was another major quest in my redefined life that I wanted to conquer to prove to myself that I could. It was definitely not easy and it took a lot of brainpower. However, once again, my unstoppable dedication kicked in and the tiny fire that I knew was burning inside of me this whole time was just re-ignited. This time, it had a bigger flame.

## Taking the First Step Without Seeing the Staircase

I began to surround myself with positive and strong-minded women, who would listen to my dreams and encourage me to take the steps to achieve them. A friend of mine introduced me to a merchant services business and encouraged me to get into it. I had absolutely no idea what it was. However, she took the time to paint the picture of what my life could look like, if I got involved with this business. She mentioned the flexibility of this job opportunity, with the potential for serious financial growth.

Since I didn't know much about the business, I let many of my insecurities stand in the way. I knew that I would love to help people and the business but I didn't want to sound like I didn't know what I was talking about. After a lot of thought and consideration, I decided that if something positive intimidated me and made me feel I wasn't ready, I needed to do it. Ready or not.

I decided to jump in headfirst. In order to be successful in this business, I needed to take a huge step out of my comfort zone. I decided that I was going to walk into a business, present myself and what I had to offer and see what would happen. I pulled into the parking lot, sat in my car and began to cry. I was very scared to do what I was about to do. However, I was even more scared of being stuck in my current situation. I sat there for a moment and had a stern talk with myself. I could either fold up and disappoint me and my kids or I could do something that might be hard now but could potentially really benefit us. I looked at myself in the mirror, dried my tears and got out of the car. I approached the business shaking like a leaf. I walked in and began to speak. Since I still had no clue what I was going to say, I jumbled over my words but still managed to muster up some sentences. From there, that first business turned into the second business, which turned into the third and fourth. I literally went to every single business that day in a two-mile strip to present my offer. With each business, I began to nail my pitch. My words became more fluent and my confidence increased. By the end of those few hours, I began to sound like I have been doing this for years.

During my business to business adventure that day, I received several rejections. However, I also received considerable interest from people who wanted to follow up. That single day had officially redefined my business and my mindset. The more I pitched to these companies about how I could help them, the more I truly began to believe I really could. Knowing where I began, I started not to care about my profit or my end result. I just truly wanted to help as many business owners, as I possibly could. As much as I knew I was helping them save money, what they didn't realize is that they were all also helping me. My merchants became my motivation.

As that business began to grow, so did my self-confidence. I was believing that I could do this and actually enjoyed doing it. I knew that I had what companies needed. Therefore, I offered it to every business owner that I came into contact with. Instead of locking my merchants into contracts, I offered them myself to keep an eye on their statements and fees and fixed anything I saw that was unfit. My "no contract approach" was how I gained most of my clients. I wanted them to feel free to leave, if I didn't deliver what I promised. My entire business then grew on trust.

Laura Ocean Solutions was created through the love I have for helping others. It offers great rates and fees on your business credit card processing and has now partnered with the most powerful business lead generator on the planet.

**How I Synced Up My Life GPS & Lessons I Learned Along the Way**

Throughout our lives, we are constantly being 'nudged' to follow certain paths. Those little nudges may scare us or make us believe we are not ready or worthy of having whatever it is that is in our heart. However, I am here to say that it is very important to tap into those nudges. What you never thought you might need, may just be on the other side of a single action. If it wasn't for my five seconds of bravery to get out of my car that day and walk into that business, I would not be where I am today or have the business that I do. The power has always been within me, even when I didn't feel it. That power is also inside of you.

The 3 lessons I learned that increased my confidence while catapulting my business:

**1.  *Just JUMP!***

If you are waiting to feel ready, you may be waiting a lifetime and depriving yourself of what you really want. Tap into the highest version of you and do what she would do. If you're scared, do it anyway! Growth is on the other side of that fear.

**2.  *Listen to You***

**Your mind is your most powerful tool**. How you speak to yourself can either positively or negatively affect your motivation.. For example, if you're telling yourself that you are not good enough or you do not know enough, you will 100% believe it, because your mind always seeks evidence to prove what you are telling it. However, if you are telling yourself that you can do whatever it is that's on your heart, your mind will seek out the evidence to also prove that thought to be true.

**3.  *If You Love What You Do, You'll Never 'Work' Another Day in Your Life***

It has, unfortunately, become very rare to hear people say that they genuinely love what they do. We are conditioned to believe that what we're *supposed* to do is go to school, get a traditional 9-5 job and make money doing that for the rest of our lives. As humans, we feel guilty for wanting something greater for ourselves or feel guilty for contemplating accepting a potential pay cut to go after whatever it is that truly sets our souls on fire. I am here to tell you that quality of life is much more important than the big paycheck. One day, when you are long gone, you will not be remembered for the amount of money you made but by the legacy that you left behind.

## God's Timing is Never Wrong

The events that take place in your life will always lead you to where you are meant to be. I don't necessarily believe that every single thing happens for a reason. However, I do believe there is meaning behind everything that takes place. I had to endure the heartbreak and lessons of those two toxic relationships to truly open my eyes to what I bring to the table and what I deserve in a relationship. Once I discovered those realizations, I was truly ready and open for real, authentic love. That is when I won the heart of world-class entertainer, Tony Ocean. When I say God's timing is never wrong, I truly mean it. I knew Tony, born Maurizio Carrara, for many years before we got together. If he and I were to date when I was still broken and really struggling, I know our outcome wouldn't have been the same. He not only won over my heart, but he won over the hearts of every person that I come with: my five kids, mom and sister. We believe that he was sent to us by my dad to pick up where he left off. He is a very gentle, kind and loving man. He was the missing puzzle piece that my family was lacking at the time. When he finally proposed, it was the easiest "yes" of my entire life.

Looking back, I also truly believe that all my business opportunities were brought into my life right when I needed them. If it wasn't for my friend showing me what my life could look like having a merchant services business, I never would have built up the courage to talk to all of those businesses that day. As a result. Laura Ocean Solutions would have never been born. They say you attract what you are ready for. After acquiring all the skills and lessons learned throughout the years, God felt that I was knowledgeable and emotionally 'open' enough to have something I could make my own. This was true, even if I didn't fully believe it at the time. I will always trust His timing over mine.

**Here's Me**

"Here's me" is a phrase that I have been saying for years, even when I don't realize that I am. That phrase is typically followed by a face full of emotion or my thoughts on whatever it is we are talking about. I've never known why I start off some sentences saying that, yet, it now has more meaning to me than ever before. To me, it means no more apologizing for being me, and no more apologizing for who I am, what I do or how I do it. With that being said, I would like to take this time to reintroduce myself:

I'm Laura. I am a mother of five, a wife, a multi-passionate individual and someone who is not afraid to take ownership of their own life. My story shaped me into the woman that I am today. I am nowhere near perfect. I'm still learning to navigate my life GPS every single day. I decided, however, to no longer compare my Chapter 1 to someone else's Chapter 10. To me, success is internal. You could have every person in the world telling you how great you are. Unless you truly believe it yourself, it's useless. Building relationships will forever be incredibly important to me, because it helps me know how I can better serve my family, friends and clients. I will no longer let fear control my outcomes and I will forever trust in the timing of the universe. Here's me: passionate, resilient and UNSTOPPABLE!

**Laura Fank-Carrara**

    Laura Fank-Carrara resides in the northwest suburbs of Chicago. She is a multi-passionate individual with several businesses that she is currently working and running. For a majority of her life, Laura has been in the service industry. Therefore, she understands just how crucial exceptional customer service is and how hard it is to come by. With that in mind, she created and owns Laura Ocean Solutions, a company in which she is dedicated to helping businesses with the most critical factors that can increase profits, by reducing credit card fees. She is a Solutions Strategist, who successfully manages a multi-million-dollar portfolio. She has been doing this for over ten years and counting. In addition to being the owner of Laura Ocean Solutions, she works at Redfin, where she holds real estate licenses in Illinois, Indiana and Missouri. However, she doesn't stop there. Laura is a Qualified Founding Affiliate with the up and coming BeeKonnected Platform. Laura's mission is to use this platform to help as many business owners as she possibly can to protect their profits and help guide entrepreneurs and businesses to more connections, world class coaching and to create strategic partnerships with leaders and influencers. Before becoming a multi-passionate entrepreneur, Laura was a single mom with five young children. She then took the leap into something that she knew absolutely nothing about. Laura's unstoppable dedication has her always looking for something more to help businesses with their particular issue or an idea that can enhance their business. She strives on being able to help her clients succeed. When Laura is not saving companies money, supporting agents at Redfin, or helping build the up and coming BeeKonnected platform, you can find her binge-watching Sex and the City reruns or traveling with her husband at his shows, redecorating a room in her house, or cuddling the family's two adorable puppies, Bella and Mia.

Laura Fank-Carrara
Laura Ocean Solutions
847-370-3370
Laura@LauraOceanSolutions.com
www.LauraOceanSolutions.com
LauraOcean.BeeKonnected.com

# Mika Bruin

## *Awakening to My Journey*

I was 24 years old when my mother passed.

I remember so vividly the night before she left us. She had been in and out of a coma for weeks. My energy was drained and my entire body aching from emotional hurt. I needed to escape if even just for a moment. I wanted a moment to breathe and to be alone with my thoughts, therefore, I decided to take a shower. When I finished, I hurried back to my mother's side. I didn't want to be away from her for long. We were huddled together at her house, waiting and watching with heart's intent.

I remember we kept trying to get her to talk, so that she would pull out of the coma. I knew in my heart that she wanted to respond, but was unable to speak due to the coma. She would look at all of us kids lovingly. The tears streaming down her face were her only way to communicate with us. It demonstrated the love she had for her children. I desperately wanted her to say something to me with the hope that things could return to normal. I couldn't imagine a world without her. She was my best friend, confidant and support. Although I was in denial, I knew she didn't have long and would be leaving us soon.

I had just stepped away only but a few minutes to speak to my aunt, when I suddenly heard my brother yell, "Mom, NO"! I bolted into the other room to join my siblings. As I witnessed my mother take her last breath, in incredulous disbelief I yelled "Mom, mom." I thought that I could wake her and bring her back to me. As the reality began to sink in, I remember the pain I felt all over my body. I wanted to vomit. I couldn't believe that I had just watched my mother take her last breath. I remember the intensity of the sadness and traumatic energy in the room. This was reflected in the shock and heartbreak of my family members and seeing their shock and heartbreak.

This nightmarish experience created anger that made me question how I was supposed to live the rest of my life. My mother was my best friend. I couldn't even begin to wrap my mind around what I had just experienced. Though I had lived the last 19 years watching her experience this pain and then watch her pass in front of me as she had.

I watched my mother struggle with cancer for 19 years. I wouldn't wish anyone to have a similar experience. I experienced many raw emotions, which had a profound impact on my life. A chain of reactions that would transpire a life awakening for me. I was so young, and I was living in the daily routine of my mother constantly being in the hospital, losing her hair, in and out of surgery… I was in hardcore denial.

It was a very difficult emotional experience to watch my mother take her last breath. It ate away at my core and created a trauma that I would continue to try to heal throughout my adult life. This feeling sucks the air from your lungs, makes the room go dark and makes you feel lost in the loss. This experience created a defense mechanism, which made it difficult for anyone to penetrate the walls that I had created. It made me physically, emotionally and mentally unable to love another person due to the fear of also losing them. This would eventually require many layers of healing to overcome.

I knew that my mother feared leaving me the most due to our relationship and how much I relied on her for everything. Therefore, it was crucial to be able to enter an awakened space, own my voice, tune in to my gifts, listen to my inner knowledge and following what my gut tells me always has been such an empowering experience.

However, at the time, I didn't know how to process what I was going through and feeling. I began to shut out the world around me. This included the people who were closest to me, such as my ex-husband. I realized that I needed to start the healing process, including the necessary inner work. While coping with her loss, my family relationships began to deteriorate, since we all had our own way of grieving. My own grief held so much anger that as the distance grew between me and them, I pushed them further away.

It was at this time that I had assumed ownership of and responsibility for my mother's nail salon. She had built it up over a 28-year period and had become the largest in Utah with a staff of over 30 people. I wanted to maintain her legacy, even though I could have sold it for a sizeable profit. I wasn't motivated by money but rather the opportunity to make her proud of me. In my heart, I knew she could see me and it meant everything to make her proud.

My decision to take over the salon could have been due to codependency. The responsibility that I assumed allowed me to ignore the pain and suppress my emotions. She was my better half in a way, and that was the one thing I had left in this physical world that tied me to her. By assuming ownership of the salon, I pushed aside all of my needs as I used it to aid me in ignoring the pain and suppressing my emotions. If I had been more in touch with my emotions, I might have questioned my reasons for doing this.

In my effort to expand my mother's business, I neglected other important parts of my life. This included key relationships as well as my marriage. Since I really didn't know how to run a business, I followed what I had seen my mother do. At the same time, I was trying to handle the emotional loss of my mother, of which I also had no idea how to manage.

As the years passed, the economy continued to grow and there was an increase in entrepreneurship. This resulted in the opening of many new nail salons with increased competition. As a result of these changes, my salon was left with very few nail technicians. The income stream slowed dramatically and we faced increased debt. The business suffered greatly and it nearly went bankrupt. By the grace of God, an offer came through to sell and I didn't hesitate to accept.

After the salon was sold, I was able to deal with my emotions and begin the healing process. I needed to repair the damaged relationships, so that the inner work could begin.

During this process, I came to realize that my marriage had spiraled out of control. We were dealing with many challenges including: declining incomes, a miscarriage, postpartum depression, and many other negative developments.

Since we were married at such a young age, we had many things to work on in order to strengthen our marriage. At the same time, I realized that I needed to work on myself. My mother had also emphasized how important that was for the success of a marriage. I had remembered my mother saying to me in a journal where she had jotted down the advice to, "Mika, no matter what, always work on you and better yourself. Marriage will have its challenge's but that's where your personal work comes in".

There were many times during my marriage that I turned off my intuitive and natural gifts. I had ignored my gut feelings about what was best for me and my children. Over and over again, I continued to ignore the promptings of that voice. I have accepted responsibility for this shortcoming and have attempted to grow as a result of that experience.

There was one particular moment that made me realize the impossibility of saving our marriage. It occurred while I was breastfeeding my baby boy. My cheeks damp and swollen from tears. The world had slowed to a minimal pace, and as I looked in his eyes my thoughts so incredulously pondered "What the hell happened"? Pain ripped through my core, almost identically as it had upon losing my mother. Life once again was unmercifully taking something from me.

I had spent the last eight years trying to get back on my feet, when the rug was pulled out from under me again. My only source of strength during this ordeal had been my wonderful children. This allowed me to hold on to a sense of insurmountable strength through everything. As you can imagine, betrayal will tear through your heart and soul. It could be compared to something as painful as death. This seemed to eat me from the inside out. My appetite declined due to the sadness. My weight and physical appearance also declined.

I did feel reassured that my intuition was right and I was able to trust in myself.

These events made me wonder "How will I manage being a single mother?" "How is it that someone with so much inner work can face these seemingly unending challenges?" I couldn't help but further question my worth in my already emotional state. I was sidelined by these events, when I thought that we had finally begun to heal our marriage. Anger and bitterness began to consume me.

Our divorce was horrible. I understand that every divorce has some negativity. However, ours seemed like a never-ending war. Luckily with the internalizing and healing, I had created and experienced with my mother's passing, I was able to process the shock and surrender myself to what was happening that was beyond my control. By sharing this, many emotions are beginning to surface.

I had to overcome a misconception that people and things created happiness. While growing up, I felt that I wasn't smart enough, the world was scary and I wasn't equipped to endure it. It was my belief that I didn't deserve to have a successful marriage and that people wouldn't accept me for who I am. I thought that happiness was created and was only dependent on my accomplishments.

These childhood experiences caused me to create unhealthy stories. This trauma continues until we recognize it and how it keeps us from realizing our full potential. These harmful patterns result in anxiety, depression, the sabotaging of beneficial relationships, addictions, and so much more. We must recognize that these are just stories. We must unravel these negative patterns from our youth, so that we can be present in the necessary moments.

This is where I really "bit the bullet" and faced my inner work journey head-on. I had heard of a course that was offered by an organization called "Landmark Worldwide." I had actually heard of it before and attended some introductory meetings before my marriage deteriorated. This is the work I had begun several years ago. This was an advanced course. They asked each person what they were hoping to gain from the course. I somehow mustered the courage to stand in front of the entire room. Even though I was crying, I shared my story.

The leader "Donna" now serves as my life "Life Coach." She mentored me and shared with what I would be learning in a brilliant and insightful way. I trusted her words and her energy. As I continued the course, although I wasn't speaking with my ex-husband at the time, I called him. In order to gain closure, I accepted responsibility for moments in which I had withheld love during our marriage. I genuinely wanted to hear him out. Our conversation allowed him to open up, and share who he had seen the woman I was and how he perceived I had shown up. It was emotionally cleansing, It was an opportunity for him to verbalize his feelings and was not intended to repair our relationship.

We apologized for those things which we both felt were selfish and out of character. It was agreed that we would try to create a friendship so that we could raise our children in a positive and in a nurturing environment. That their lives would never lack in love. We would not focus on the past and what had transpired, but that our children were our most important responsibility. We wanted our children to know that their parents only had their best interests in mind. Those twenty minutes of conversation changed our lives. It was a very empowering experience.

Once our relationship ended, it allowed me to begin to realize my full potential as a woman. It is almost like I had a rebirth . I got to truly step into my vulnerability in a way I never had before. It was learning that it's okay to not always be okay and your ability to admit that to yourself and others. Being able to take precious "me" time, and slowing down and experiencing things that were really natural to who I am.

During this period, I had a wonderful community of people who supported me. I get emotional thinking about all the love around me, to be honest, I was taken back during my separation with all the amazing family and friends in my life, and I continue to experience so much support. I will be forever grateful to this group of family and friends who supported me.

In retrospect, I can't imagine what would have happened if we hadn't had that unity. We all have choices and a sense of responsibility in every situation. We have all faced circumstances in our life that are beyond our control. However, we assume the responsibility for handling them in the best way possible. If a relationship doesn't work out, it is up to you to make decision to go with the flow. You must take the necessary steps to free yourself of the pain and the emotions that you are experiencing, so that you can create the life that you want. For me, the life I've chosen is to embrace the universally beautiful gift my children are, and the love I have for them. I am also inspired by their love for me as their mother. It has given me the solid foundation, so that I can become more self-aware in all areas of my life. My children have allowed me to stay present and aware of their needs. As a result, I always show up as I refuse to allow myself to show up any less than the best version of who I am, with my raw emotions, and no sugarcoating. This provides my children with an example of strength and the need to show up as ourselves. Although my children are the central focus of my life, their love showed me that I can use my gifts to do more. This is a calling that would provide me with a steady income, and to show up in my authentic self and raise them powerfully.

Our lives can be divided into phases that teach us about life. There are layers that allow us the to heal and expand our awareness. There will be moments when the only option is to shift. I have experienced many of these moments. One of these shifts occurred during my separation. The chaos was proof that my marriage no longer worked and the reality was that I needed to take control.

These moments were critical for my growth and have contributed to making me the woman I am today. There is an analogy that I love to use about an onion. Each person has many layers to peel back that we are taught by our families. We need to peel back these layers, so we can become the person that we want to be. I truly believe those things which we are taught and retain in our youth by our family, that we have layers and layers to peel back that could be likened to that of patterns created, and as we peel back these layers we continue to expand, growing into the person we so earnestly strive to create. We are clearing a path to experience and embrace, to blossom that true greatness we were meant to. Please, I'm imploring you to be cognizant of the fact that it must be created. I took everything in my life, and I found a way to grow from it. I'd peel back another layer, embrace an eye-opening moment, and then another and another. A beautifully never-ending cycle. They say "The teacher appears when the student is ready", and I believe that to be true without a doubt.

While we can't control the life's circumstances, we can choose whether or not we heal from it. Grief is a natural process. We are very capable of dealing with what we face. During my separation when I was so consumed in my heartache, that I was also full of self-loathing and pity. Many people during my separation tried to increase my self-awareness, by asking if I was actually happy in my marriage. My response was that my marriage had nothing to do with my happiness. I had done so much inner work at this time, which I had healed so much that I needed to. Although there were serious problems with my marriage was facing turmoil, I was truly happy with who I was and what I was becoming.

Although I have experienced many other emotions, happiness is an internal experience. Despite the problems in my marriage, it didn't mean that I couldn't be happy. I remember someone asking, "well don't you feel broken now", amidst my separation as if I was a victim of sorts. I had glanced at him almost in disbelief and confidently responded with, "No, I'm not broken. I am hurt". The breakup of my marriage was upsetting. However, I am now over that experience and it no longer has power over me.

It was necessary to be responsible, forgive, and create a relationship, in order to show our children what successful co-parenting is like.

Many years later, I'm enjoying raising my children and am truly kicking ass at raising them. While some days rock my world, others are easy and I'm able to go with the flow. I have learned what to do and when to ask for help. It is difficult to accept my vulnerability and is now becoming more comfortable and natural.

It is important to be aware of your feelings and to effectively deal with any pain, sadness or other emotion that you are dealing with. However, you must recognize what that emotion is. It is important to have a select group of people to communicate with and provide support through this process.

I have found that this group I communicate with has supported me in facing every challenge that I have faced. This group should include close friends who you can undoubtedly trust to share your most vulnerable and traumatic moments with. These people will be crucial in helping you reach your higher self. If you can set a daily routine to be present, and aware of these support systems, it'll shift your way of being so much so that'll you'll take action required to make those necessary dramatic shifts.

When those moments present themselves, you must show up and make the decision to act. These events unfold powerfully. Some of the strongest and most successful people made a decision and acted on it. You must find simple tools that provide you support or growth, which must be practiced every day.

I am able to find so much peace and clarity when I commit to meditate daily. During the chaos that I experienced; it shifted my life drastically. I was helped by the power of meditation, mixed with the use of essential oils and having a life coach. When this was combined with my growing sense of worth as a woman and mother, it resulted in a powerful shift that continues to honor me.

This growing confidence has given me clarity about my future. I have learned that the words we use are beautiful and powerful. This has given me the ability to be truly happy and free. I understand my imperfections and I understand that I do not need to be perfect.

I am now aware that I have a bigger purpose and a more powerful calling.

However, I had lost that because of everything that I have gone through. I am now aware of my power and my ability to deal with anything that I am faced with in life. We are meant to make an impact on others, and the only way to do that is if we continue to keep unraveling that onion layer at a time. It is important to me to continue to unravel the onion layers on a daily basis for myself, my kids and for the world. You need to be creative on what you want to try to become. This applies to my role as a mother and my relationships and friendships. If we do this, it will inspire others to do the same. Trust the universe and the process, as it'll allow you to surrender.

In my podcast, I love to share parts of my story that will make a difference for all my listeners. It has provided a space for connection, healing, and powerful insights. It lets me be the voice that allows others to see what's possible, by relating in a powerful way.

I believe that we were all meant to make a difference in this world, in our own way. This means that you must own your voice, speak up, let your voice be heard and dropping all judgments about yourself and others.

You have the ability to be present to what is happening in your life, accept you're the responsibility and steer your life in the direction you want it to go. I love the saying "It goes the way I say," which my coach taught me. There is power in our words because we create what we say and it goes the way we say it to be.

In my life as a single mother, I will juggle raising these tiny littles, running successful businesses and dating. I will also continue to show up every day and stay in conversations that will create so many insights that I can use to look within and take action on.

We have ideas on what life should be like, based on what we have seen or have been told. Therefore, when things go in a different direction, we panic and feel like we have lost control over our lives. However, it is necessary to work through those challenges. It should become an opportunity to accept responsibility for how you say that your life is going to be. If you look with within and try to gain insight, you will become a better human being. So, self-reflect always and know the challenging times will pass. Fuel your mind with insightful content to better you as a human being. I strive to make a difference in the life of others by sharing my story, and the stories of others. I hope that you will accept my challenge to grow your mind, by listening to my podcast and find stories that resonate with you.

Check out Episode 45 to hear more about my story and how I'm continually implementing specific tools in my life to keep expanding as a woman.

I'd love for you to connect with me here: https://linktr.ee/mikajbruin

Podcast link https://podcasts.apple.com/us/podcast/inspired-babes-lets-chat/id1497584474

Mika Bruin

# Mika Bruin

Mika Bruin is a passionate podcaster, wellness advocate, successful entrepreneur, mother of three, lover of laughter and much more. Although she dreamed of being an Olympic ice skater or gymnast, the universe had an even brighter and more influential future for her.

Her career began at 18, when she worked as a receptionist at her mother's nail school. This sparked an interest in attending nail school, which then led her to work in the nail industry for more than 10 years. At the age of 24, her mother and best friend, the light of her life, left this world. Upon her mother's passing, she took over the salon, which she operated and managed for the next two years, before selling in 2012.

Her mother had been a very nurturing inspiration in her life. As Mika watched her over the years, she admired her mother's hard work, which allowed her to achieve success. She was particularly impressed when she gave advice. This is because she actually listened to those who spoke to her. She was always fully present and authentic, even while enduring her trials.

As Mika overcame challenges and found peace with the passing of her mother, it create a shift in her life that would lead her on her destined path. Moments took place in her personal life, that lead her to see more natural avenues of healing. She discovered the incredible properties of essential oils, which she shares with others due to her own successful use.

In February 2020, she launched her podcast "Inspired Babes — Let's Chat". For years, those close to her have presented her with the idea of beginning her own Youtube channel or podcast. The idea really didn't resonate with her, until a friend shared his own podcast. This provided Mika with the idea to create an outlet of diversity, where she could empower those with different life experiences, feelings and ambitions. Everyone who shared their stories to empower and heal those who listened.

As an empath, and someone who embraces all wholesome and loving things, Mika thrives because of her ability to see people for who they are to their very soulful cores. She not only sees their potential but also stands by their side to give them strength in finding their power to be raw and vulnerable. This will allow them to live passionate and creative lives, so they know that they are not alone on this life's journey.


Mika Bruin
Mika Fiack LLC
801-502-8780
Mika.InspiredByOils@gmail.com
linktr.ee/MikaJBruin

# Amber Champagne-Matos

## *Beauty in the Breakdown*

I write my dreams in pencil. It is not so they can be erased, but because they can always be revised.

Before I tragically lost my second son, Linus, I thought I had my dream job.

I was a U.S. Senior Educator for Benefit Cosmetics. For almost five years, I traveled the country extensively, trained thousands of other estheticians, and helped to write groundbreaking educational content for the company at large.

Understandably, this job was highly sought after. I filled one of only 16 elite positions in the country and one of maybe only 40 or 50 positions (depending on the time) in all of the world!

I was given development beyond my wildest dreams. I was in some kind of high caliber training and development session at least once every six months. I was chosen to go to an unforgettable luxury training put on by LVMH (Louis Vuitton Moet Hennessy owns Benefit) in the Napa Valley. I even did SPARK Leadership training with Angie Morgan herself.

I attended work parties at Domaine Chandon, the Skydeck in Chicago, the Monarch Beach Resort and many other incredibly lavish locations throughout the country. I was given a Louis Vuitton gift card for my three year anniversary. I went on a special private tour of the Grand Ole Opry and got to sing a Patsy Cline song on the stage. I worked with social media influencers, wrote video scripts and did many other things.

It was an amazing job, my dream job I thought, and quite frankly, it was pretty glamorous.

However, losing a child is one of those absolutely devastating things that will make you question *everything* and put you back in touch with who you really are. At my core, I am a wild and free-spirited Enneagram 4. I am an individualist, who likes to do things my own way and has a passion for helping others.

Corporate life never quite suited me. I didn't like to be told how to dress, act or speak. I didn't love how some people tore others down to try and prop themselves up. Parts of my identity felt unwillingly chained to my job and I always felt like the odd woman out.

At the time of my devastating loss, I had recently left Benefit. I didn't know how I would continue to do that job with a baby, so I took another corporate position heading culture and education at a tech company. I hated it. I wanted to leave, but I didn't know how.

Losing Linus helped me to see how precious and unpredictable life really is. I realized that I shouldn't waste one more second in a place I wasn't in love with. I needed to spend my time pursuing my true passions.

Therefore, I decided to find the beauty in the breakdown and rewrite my dreams.

Since esthetics school, I had yearned to open my own business and create my own skincare line. However, I didn't even know where to start. It is very daunting to think about breaking through the intense marketing of huge conglomerates, like Estee Lauder, L'oreal, and LVMH and gaining exposure. I had firsthand knowledge of what goes on behind the scenes of these major skincare and cosmetic companies. They have huge teams working around the clock, to ensure that they rank at the top of Google. Honestly, it seemed unachievable, so I never started.

However, after walking through the most difficult season in my life to date, nothing seemed impossible anymore. With a visceral passion for helping go-getters to reach their skin goals for good and a credit card, I ventured out on my own into the world of business and started Brows on Main and Prohibition Skin.

I wanted my brand to not only impact the lives of those directly using the products and services but also impact the lives of our nation's youth. As the mother of a teenager, I truly believe in guiding, molding and supporting the next generation, so they can go on to do great things. Therefore, from day one I dedicated 10% of my total proceeds to supporting local youth organizations. I haven't looked back once. In just nine months, during COVID and all, we were in the black! Praise God!

I know it might sound frivolous, but when I was really going through it all, doing my skincare routine (especially after crying for long periods of time) always made me feel just a little bit better; a little more human. The water felt cooling and healing. The scents of my favorite products helped me to relax. The motions made me feel grounded. The results gave me the confidence to go out into the world, even though I often felt like I was dying inside.

That's why I want to help as many people as possible. I know and love that there is healing and confidence taking place in every client interaction. It is sometimes much more than what can be seen on the surface.

I now have a couple more secrets to share with you.

First, did you know that esthetics school only teaches you how to pass the state exam? Yes, my friend, it's true. As an esthetics school graduate, you mostly depart with a sufficient knowledge about your state's sanitation laws. You definitely don't know everything you're ever going to know (or even a fraction of what you'll come to know) about skin science and skincare.

You have to work diligently and consistently to specialize in an area that interests you, which is what I've done for nearly a decade. I have done extensive research on what I've now called "*The Mid-Life Skin Crisis*". It is funny how a challenging situation can even help you find a name for something you've been working on.

When I was in my late 20's, I began getting cystic acne. Prior to that, had I played the game "Never have I ever" and someone said "Never have I ever had acne"… I would've been able to steer clear from drinking. And phew…

because I really don't drink (it's not good for your skin), so I'd be in trouble!

Growing up, I had 99 problems. However, my skin wasn't one. After I had my first son, things changed drastically. In discussing these late-in-life breakouts with others, I noticed that many people were having the same issues. However, when trying to find good solutions, I was coming up short.

There are many products created specifically for acne-ridden teens and older people who are trying to defy aging, but there is less out there for people trying to combat both concurrently. However, in my experience and in doing market research, I've found there are many people, especially women between the ages of 35 and 44, who are constantly searching for ways to tackle both anti-aging and acne simultaneously.

I, therefore, decided that I would do something about it.

I learned everything I could about dual-action active ingredients, cosmetic chemistry and nutrition. I tried many different products myself to see what was most effective and what wasn't. I worked with many clients dealing with similar issues and garnered their feedback. I became an expert in dealing with midlife skin and I continue to learn each and every day.

Are you wondering if you are dealing with a midlife skin crisis?

**Here Are Some Signs You Might Be:**

1. You find yourself staring at yourself in the mirror or (dare I say it?) pulling out the magnifying mirror. You often notice "new" fine lines, patches of hyperpigmentation and/or redness and sensitivity.

2. You're well beyond your teen years, but you are still getting breakouts (especially in the jawline). You keep trying to dry them out or pop them to get them to go away. Nevertheless, they keep rearing their ugly heads, like it's a never-ending game of whack-a-mole.

3. Every product you try seems like it "doesn't work, so you keep trying new things. You just switched up your cleanser a week ago, but you're not seeing any results yet. You complained to your friend Sally and

she said to try Cleanser X because it *definitely* works. So, you're off to your local beauty store again.

Sound like you? No worries! You are not alone. Luckily for all of us, when it comes to skin, a few lifestyle changes, and the right products for your skin, will get you glowing in no time.

Please note that crucially important piece which says, *"your skin"*. Everyone is completely different and, therefore, often need very individualized, custom solutions.

Here's what to do. Let's work backwards from above:

1. **Stop listening to Sally. Just because something worked for her, doesn't mean it's going to work for you. Remember, "your skin" are the keywords here!**

First and foremost, I encourage you to work with a professionally licensed esthetician who specializes in skin like yours. It will definitely be worth your time to discuss your skin issues, goals and desired results with someone who can easily point you in the right direction and get you started on a custom skincare regimen that will truly give you results.

There will be no more guessing games at your local Sephora!

It will also be really helpful to have someone along for the ride, who can help you to stay consistent with your routine for the right amount of time and change things up, only when they might need to be changed.

2. **Stop trying to be Dr. Pimple Popper. I mean, don't stop watching it because, quite frankly, it's amazing, but stop picking at your face.**

Exfoliation and Vitamin C are your besties.

When it comes to break outs and cell turnover (hello anti-aging!), exfoliation is crucial. However, you have to make sure you're using something that is not only effective but also gentle, since you'll likely need to use it pretty regularly. You might have to use it almost daily, depending on the level of your breakouts. A combination of a good, anti-aging acidic exfoliating blend and gentle manual exfoliant works best.

Vitamin C is an incredibly powerful antioxidant that not only helps you to keep breakouts at bay, but can keep your skin healthy, vibrant and youthful. It also helps with acne scarring and other forms of hyperpigmentation!

When choosing a Vitamin C product, take care to find a more stable form of Vitamin C and use those products within two to three months. Once Vitamin C products are opened, they begin to oxidize. Oxidation makes a product less effective in the long run, so don't be afraid to slather that Vitamin C all over your skin, friend!

3. **Stop looking in the mirror so much and definitely stay away from the infamous magnifying mirror.**

Spend that time meal prepping or learning more about nutrition. Diet is key. Although we don't likely walk through each day thinking about it, our skin is an organ. In fact, it's the largest organ of our body and it operates like one. Ensuring that your daily water intake is fulfilled and eating as clean as possible are vital to our skin's health and functionality.

Taking these practical steps can help you to get the results you've been searching for.

If you want to understand your skin and what it's going through in a more in-depth way, check out my complimentary e-book "An Esthetician's Guide to The Mid-Life Skin Crisis" by going to browsonmain.com.

Life is precious. Don't waste it searching for skincare products or staring in the mirror wondering what's happening. Let a seasoned professional do what they love, so you can get back to confidently living your life and enjoying time with your loved ones.

And friend, most importantly, if you've found yourself in a place where you don't love every minute of what you're doing, what are you waiting for? Go pursue your passions. Follow your dreams. Know that it is OK to revise them as you go. Become the woman you were always meant to be. Don't let a damn thing stand in your way.

## Amber Champagne-Matos

Amber Champagne-Matos, the owner and founder of Brows on Main and Prohibition Skin, believes in doing what you love; not what you once loved. Amber is a licensed esthetician, skincare entrepreneur, and former U.S. Educator for Benefit Cosmetics! During her career with Benefit, she traveled the country extensively, trained thousands of other estheticians, and became one of the first-ever National Senior Educators. Amber also also wrote groundbreaking educational content for the company, both nationally and internationally, assisting Benefit in successfully implementing and executing exceptional internal development programs and client-facing product education. This contributed to their remarkable corporate growth. To put that in perspective, Benefit is one of the fastest-growing major players in the beauty industry employing more than 6,000 estheticians world-wide. Benefit does business in 59 countries across five continents and is part of the world-renowned luxury brand, Louis Vuitton. Her experience with this major cosmetics brand gave her the edge and knowledge she needed to confidently face the world of beauty and dare to dream. She opened her own business, created a beauty blog, and has an up and coming skincare line. Since opening Brows on Main, she has helped many women overcome what she has now called "The Midlife Skin Crisis."

Amber currently resides in Southern California with her husband Tony and son Liam. Although she lives in California, she considers herself truly "East Coast" at heart, is fascinated by the Enneagram (she's a 4w5 with strong 3 tendencies), and once did makeup during New York's famous fashion week. To learn more about the Midlife Skin Crisis and how to conquer anti-aging and acne simultaneously, go to www.browsonmain.com.

Amber Champagne-Matos
Brows on Main and Prohibition Skin
21372 Brookhurst Street, Unit 233
Huntington Beach, CA 92646
714-655-7630
BrowsonMain@gmail.com
www.BrowsonMain.com

# Joyce Wietrecki

## *When Life Changes in a Moment, Hang On!*

### Brady Bunch is not Real Life

Growing up in my household was a character-building experience. It was nothing like the '*Brady Bunch*' series on TV. Like many people, my childhood left a lot to be desired. At 10 years old, I was making the meals because I wanted to be able to eat and doing my own laundry, so I'd have clean clothes for school. As the oldest of six kids, I was responsible for taking care of myself and my siblings. What I learned at an early age was to be self-sufficient. I never understood why my mom had six kids because she never seemed happy or interested in what we were doing.

My grandparents had a huge positive impact on my life. They were great role models, who showed us what unconditional love was. I treasured Wednesdays because my grandmother would come over to help mom out. We would race home from school on those days because we knew grandma would have a hot lunch waiting for us with a warm smile. We had fun with grandma learning how to bake, cook and other life lessons. We adored my grandparents because they spent time with us and showered us with lots of love.

My grandfather taught me how to plant a garden, shared wonderful stories and described ways to succeed in life. Little did I know that these words of wisdom would be the lifeline I would cling to through the tough times. My rocky childhood prepared me for life's challenges that I never imagined I would learn to overcome.

My grandparents would pop in twice a week with little treats and take us for ice cream and to Kiddieland amusement park. My grandparents were my mentors and were instrumental in helping me develop my foundational values, goals, and dreams.

When I was twelve years old, I decided that I would be a successful businesswoman by the time I was 30 years old. I created posters of the sayings my grandpa taught me. I hung those posters in my room and read them every day. He was my inspiration to keep trying when facing obstacles. There sure were a lot of them during my formative years. When he died, my parents were paralyzed with grief. He was the captain of the ship and without him, they were tossed into stormy waters without a compass. What I realize now was that God was developing my fortitude to prepare me for my future challenges.

## When the Going Gets Tough, the Tough Get Going

A year and a half later, when my little brother died at two-years-old, our family was shattered. Instead of bringing my parents together and appreciating the five remaining children, they sank into the depths of depression and numbed themselves with alcohol. I realized that I had to focus on how to help myself. I threw myself into school. Teachers saw something special in me and praised me for things I did well. I focused all of my energies on school and explored what I could do with my life.

It was from the solid foundation which my grandparents nurtured in me, that the seeds of a strong character were established. It helped me survive the verbal abuse I received from my mom, who would say to me: *"Who do you think you are?"* *"You can't go to that school because we don't have the money."* These words beat down my confidence and made me feel as if I wasn't worthy or smart enough to achieve my dreams.

## Where There's a Will There's a Way

In high school, my English teacher, Ms. Russell, encouraged me to join the student council. The next year she said I should run for president of the student council. I was terrified, but she insisted I would be a great leader. I wrote an essay for my campaign and won the election! During my senior year in high school, I was president of the student council, a member of the National Honor Society, took AP Biology and was in the concert choir. It was a fantastic year!

After attending community college for a year, I entered the University of Illinois at Champaign to pursue my dreams. I was excited, yet terrified at the same time. I was finally away from my parents and embarking on a new adventure. When my scholarship money ran out, I came back to Chicago to figure out what to do with my life. My husband and I decided to start a family and I had a baby girl. I was thrilled to be a mother!

**What Doesn't Kill You Makes You Stronger**

A year later on Halloween, there was a knock on my door. Our best friends came to tell me that my husband was killed in a work accident. To say I was devastated, was an understatement. We had only been married four years and were just beginning our lives. I didn't know what to do and walked around in a daze for weeks. Thank goodness for my daughter, because she was my reason for living. I began looking for ways to support her. A friend introduced me to a business that allowed me to work from home. I went to meetings to learn how to build my new business, networked with positive people and began to carve out new dreams. I began dating and was married to my high school sweetheart a year later. Life looked like it was turning around for me.

My life with my second husband was wonderful. We soon had a son and our happy family did fun things together. We enjoyed being involved in our children's extracurricular activities. I served on the school boards and was active in our church, chairing various committees. I was thankful every day for this family.

They say don't get too comfortable because things could change in a moment. You see, I was to be faced with another catastrophe. My second husband was injured in a near-fatal skiing accident, while we were on a weekend ski trip for our son's birthday. What started as a fun weekend adventure turned into a nightmare. He was rushed to the hospital in a rural area and underwent

5 ½ hours of leg surgery in which he was given a blood transfusion because he lost so much blood during the surgery. My husband died once on the operating table and thankfully they were able to revive him. While we waited in the ER during that surgery, I had this sense of foreboding and knew that our life would be changed forever.

## Failure is Not an Option!

You never know how you will react in a tragedy, until you are faced with one. That's when you discover the depth of your character. While my husband was trying to survive in and out of the hospital for seven months, I was fighting with the medical team to find a better solution. When they couldn't stop the infection after five months of I.V. antibiotics, the doctors stated that the only solution left was to amputate his left leg. I told them that was unacceptable and my fierce protective side emerged. I was not accepting failure. I sought out another orthopedic surgeon, who was willing to try a new procedure.

The second surgeon knew of an innovative procedure using stainless steel pins to secure the bones in place, while allowing the leg to heal. That surgery was successful. Over the next 18 months, my husband went through the long road to recovery to learn how to walk again and how to live with a new, different leg that had many limitations. He learned to triumph over tragedy.

## You Can Do Anything You Set Your Mind to Do

To add to the actual trauma, while he was laid up from all those surgeries, there was also the trauma of no income. I woke up one morning in stark terror realizing that now, I was solely responsible for the financial support of my family. I had no clue how I was going to do it. Things looked very bleak and I was in desperate need of a job. A friend approached me, said her husband had a job opening in his department. She wondered if I would be interested. I jumped for joy because my prayers were answered!

When I first received the call offering me the job as a supervisor, I was excited and frightened at the same time. I gave myself a pep talk, was determined to start the role with enthusiasm and focused on making a positive difference.

The CFO asked me to lead the accounts payable staff. My first assignment was to develop a collaborative team. On that first day when I walked through the sea of cubicles and met my staff, I realized that I was intimidated by them. Here I was, a young woman with a staff old enough to be my mother. *What could I teach them?* I've realized since then is that they were probably just as intimidated by me. *What would I ask them to do? Would I be demanding them to change their routine? Would I ask them to work longer hours?* I put my experience from my business and leading others in volunteer programs to work and created a plan to lead this new team. I learned that it takes more than knowing the technical skills to be a good supervisor. It requires building a relationship, developing trust and finding ways to engage them.

## You Can Get Bitter or Get Better

I would often doubt my ability. Those old fears and negative words from my mom would come back to haunt me. I remembered the positive sayings my grandfather encouraged me to focus on, said my affirmations and worked at improving my leadership skills. I learned new programs to increase my skills and attended workshops to become a better leader. I learned to sharpen my decision-making and how to negotiate with others. Through this discovery stage, I found that I had more strength, courage and resilience than I ever imagined.

When I was at that first company, I pursued a new direction and transferred into the corporate university. This was where I discovered my natural talent for training. The Vice President of Learning and Development supported my decision to go back to college to earn my B.A. degree in Adult Learning. Amazingly, I completed my degree in two years, while working a full-time job. I soon realized I had outgrown my role in that company and it was time to move on. I began seeking other opportunities and was referred to another Fortune 500 company as a Training Director. Working on the team at the corporate university prepared me for this new role in the financial services industry.

After a few years, I became an AVP heading up Learning and Development at a large community bank and expanded their training program from simple teller training to a robust multi-faceted program that included leadership development, retail sales management, commercial lending and mortgage training. I simultaneously began working on my M.A. degree in Organizational Leadership. I was accepted into De Paul University, the one I wanted to attend when I first decided to pursue my college education in high school. Another dream was realized.

## Count Your Blessings

When I look back on my career, I realize that I achieved many of the goals I wrote down on my dream board. I kept my eye on the goals, visualized where I wanted to be and read my affirmations daily to keep my attitude positive. I surrounded myself with successful leaders, refined my leadership style and learned how to influence others.

When the going got tough, I'd think about what my grandfather told me and think about how far I have come. One of the other things he said was to, "Count my blessings, no matter how difficult the situation." We always have something to be thankful for.

Today, I read affirmations and keep a gratitude journal focusing on the positives in my life. I challenge you to write down your dreams, look at them every day and learn from each challenge. I share my story to inspire you, that no matter what challenges you have faced, you can overcome them and achieve your dreams. Never give up!

# Joyce Wietrecki

Joyce managed her own home business for 15 years, where she learned success principles from authors like Ken Blanchard, Jack Canfield, Dale Carnegie, Rich DeVos, Napoleon Hill, Og Mandino, John Maxwell and Zig Ziglar. These great authors helped to provide her the foundation of sound business principles. Reading their words of wisdom guided her path to creating an action plan to achieve her dreams.

When faced with finding a job to support her family after a life-changing event, she took a deep breath and jumped into Corporate America. She applied the leadership principles that she had learned to become a manager in the corporate arena.

After 25 years in a corporate position, she took the plunge and started her own consulting business. As CEO of her own venture, Corporate Training

Group, Inc., Joyce works with Fortune 500 companies in the consumer goods, retail, and financial services industries. She helps organizations identify solutions to retain high performing employees, create programs to increase productivity and develop leaders to generate sustainable results. She has a proven track record of transforming managers into extraordinary leaders. As a seasoned executive in Corporate America, Joyce specializes in leadership development, performance management and emotional intelligence. Her talent management expertise has been in high demand from blue-chip companies, like AbbVie, American Bar Association, Kraft Heinz Company, Newell Rubbermaid, Reynolds Consumer Products, and Walgreens.

Joyce is a graduate of DePaul University, Chicago, IL, from which she holds a B.A. degree in Adult Learning and a M.A. degree in Organizational Leadership. She has served as a Professional Advisor at DePaul University, President of the Chicago Chapter for the Association for Talent Development and on the National Board of Leadership Development for ATD. She is an NSA Speakers Academy graduate and speaks to groups about transformational leadership. She is also a Certified Professional Coach.

Joyce A. Wietrecki, MA, CPC
Corporate Training Group, Inc.
2 N. Elm Street
Mount Prospect, IL 60656
Joyce@ctg.us.com
www.ctg.us.com
www.linkedin.com/in/JoyceWietrecki

# Marilynn Reis Sonier

## *The Answer Was Always There... It Was ME*

I had convinced myself that life was good. Every morning I would go in and get my daughter when she woke up. I'd slowly walk into her room, taking each step very dramatically. She would giggle, which was the cutest little sound that I had ever heard, then she would turn to hide and bury herself in the blankets. I'd tickle her and make her laugh and laugh. I'd give her a moment to wake up and I'd just watch her, so in love. That cute little face stirred something in me. There was nothing in the world that filled my heart with such pure joy. I'd pick her up out of her crib and hug her and kiss her. I'd ask her how she slept and we'd head downstairs to get "milkies." She was my "why."

I spent every morning with her. I didn't start my workday, until I put her down for her nap. I had convinced myself that I did this because I owned my business and I was in control of my days. Looking back, it's embarrassingly clear that I just didn't want to start working.

One day, just like any other day, after spending my morning with my daughter, I put her down for a nap and headed down to my office. Where was I going to start? I had tried to ignore it and to pretend I was in control. However, the anxiety that I had most mornings while I played with my daughter, finally had my full attention. I was buried in a to do list that was a mile long. Emails had already flooded my inbox in the few short hours of the morning. I had already missed a call from my general manager, and I knew I didn't want to start with that voicemail. Whatever she was calling to tell me about would have to wait. Honestly, I was over it, all of it.

I was sitting there at my desk, just staring at my computer. I was thinking about all the things I had to do and all the bills that had to be paid. Mostly, it was worrying. Worrying about all the ways that all of it could go wrong. Was it ever going to get any better?

Then it hit me, out of nowhere, "what the fuck am I doing?!"

In that moment, it became crystal clear. I didn't like my life... at all.

And even worse, I thought to myself, I don't even know who I am... this is not me.

The thoughts didn't stop there. The hopelessness engulfed me. Cue all the despair. I started to reflect on the past ten years. I was ashamed that I didn't have more to show for all my hard work and sacrifice. Over the past five years, I'd opened a string of gaming parlors. A new, lucrative industry had lured me in. All I could see was dollar signs. I was determined to do better and build on my previous mistakes. Before that, I had opened my first business, a salon and spa. It was the day after my 26th birthday and I was fresh out of beauty school. I had stars in my eyes and a fire in my belly. I was very brave, but incredibly naïve. The reality check came fast and hard. I didn't have a clue about the real world, how to make money, or how to run a business. I had no idea how many businesses failed. I worked my ass off for five years, but I never got it to be the successful business I wanted it to be.

So I sat there, pregnant, rubbing my belly and wallowing at my desk. I couldn't deny that I had experienced some growth. I was playing a much bigger game. After all, I had built a brand from the ground up and expanded it to four locations in three years. I was making more money, I was running a much bigger business and I was working on my schedule. From the outside looking in, things looked pretty good. I had convinced myself that life was good. Looking back, it's easy to see why. It's the story we're sold, work hard and you'll succeed. So, why didn't this feel like success? It wasn't fulfilling, and my freedom was a total illusion. What good was more money and being my own boss, if it meant I was working all the time, didn't enjoy my work and was too stressed out to enjoy myself when I wasn't working? Until that moment, I had never stopped to think about it.

I could feel my dreams slipping away. Maybe it was because I was pregnant, but in that moment I realized if I didn't find the courage to change my life, I would end up another struggling small business owner with only a false sense of pride to comfort my ego. What about all the people who had supported me through the years, through the endless tears and through the endless inspiration? They had also lived this emotional rollercoaster, just by supporting me, and I wasn't going to let them down.

I was done telling myself how smart I was, how much potential I had and how I'd create this incredible life for my children. I was ready to start living that. I had no idea where to begin, of course. I just knew there was much more for me than this stress-filled version of success. So, that was it. I was done! As cliché as it sounds, I felt like an enormous weight had been lifted. I was going to sell my business immediately.

If I'm being honest, that excitement was short lived. I put a plan to sell into action, but what was next? How was it going to be different? I had a relatively easy first trimester with my daughter, but I was a mess this time around. I was tired, sick and super hormonal. It was not an ideal time to throw caution to the wind. I went headfirst into a depressive tailspin. Pity-party, table for one, please? I mean really, was now the time to shut off my income? I was pregnant! How the heck was I going to start a new business?

This was crazy! I was scared. Believe me, I was terrified! Yet, I could feel in my gut that it was now or never. I wasn't sure of anything else, but I knew this was the first step to freedom. It was the first step to getting my life back.

I pulled up my big girl pants and embarked on a very private, soul-searching journey. I needed to explore who I was and who I wanted to be. I spent months thinking about this. Who did I want to be? What did my dream life look like? What legacy did I want to leave? Why did I want it?

Deciding to sell that business gave me another chance at my best life. However, my life didn't truly change, until the day that I understood on a deep level that if I wanted a different life, I was going to have to change. That was the most important lesson I could have ever learned, and I want to share it with you.

The truth is that the answers were inside of me the whole time.

It's not an easy thing to accept that we create our worlds. We have unlimited potential, but it is our deep down beliefs that hold us back and keep us stuck. It is such a disappointing realization to know that all of our struggles and apparent failures are due to our own self-imposed limits. You don't want to accept that deep down you believe you are so undeserving. It's the truth whether you are ready to hear it or not. Your world and your current reality, is a reflection of how you see yourself. It's this same understanding, however, that affords you the opportunity to finally create the life you've been longing for.

If any of this resonates with you, if you feel like you could be doing more, if you're tired of feeling stuck, tired of the same results no matter how hard you work, tired of being stressed out, tired of being so damn tired... if you want more fulfillment, more freedom and more happiness, you have to change on the inside. If you want to change your life, you need to change your thinking. You have to ask yourself what you truly want. You have to fall madly and deeply in love with yourself. You also need to let go of all the fears, expectations, opinions, doubts and worries that are keeping you from shining your light on the world.

I spent months thinking. I thought about what I wanted for my life. I found that really understanding why I wanted it was the fuel to my fire. I started waking up every day with an unbridled enthusiasm and energy. I couldn't wait to dig deeper into my development. I was literally waking up before my 5:30 am alarm, six months pregnant, barely able to contain my excitement... I woke up with purpose, I was working towards my goals. How would you like that for your life? Are you tired of pressing snooze every day?

If you can see it in your mind and you believe it in your heart, you will create it in reality.

Once you know what you want, you've got to believe you can have it. We've got beliefs deep down that guide our behavior and lead to self-sabotage. This is why you always feel stuck. It is why you're always getting the same results. It is why you plateau and nothing you do seems to work, no matter how hard you work. There's a difference between knowing something and truly believing it and living it. You may know you are worthy and deserving, but it's the pesky beliefs that have been wired in our brains that guide our behavior. They tell a different story. You need to love yourself before anything else in your life will work. Once I understood this, I was able to start improving my self-image. For the first time I started prioritizing myself. This included my health, my goals and my feelings. Every single day now, I wake up and I think about my goals with full faith that I can achieve them.

Success can never be achieved in the shadows of doubt and fear.

If you're getting cozy with the idea that this is esoteric "woo-woo" stuff and that you don't have the power to change your life, that you're not responsible for it and that you're a victim of poor circumstance, stop right now. This is science, neuroscience specifically. If you want more for your life, it's time to get uncomfortable... it is time to wake up!

Once I understood this, I was able to stop playing the victim. I took responsibility for all that my life was. I realized there was a success switch that I needed to flip on. I let go of any and all expectations. I was done worrying about what everyone else thought about me and what I was doing. I stopped focusing on everything that could go wrong. I started thinking about all that could go right! I rewrote my story, by looking for all the good in it, instead of focusing on the challenges and hard times. I didn't erase the struggles though. I made a decision to appreciate them for all the strength of character and resiliency they had built in me. My life was like a painting. For years, I stared at it thinking it was a mess. Once I shifted my perspective, I saw it as a beautiful mess, and today it's my message.

Success and happiness aren't linear, like we're taught to believe. We are way too comfortable with "impossible," and in a really bad relationship with failure. We should be taught to embrace failure, instead of fearing it. You aren't a failure, until you quit. So I beg of you, don't stop! If you're reading this, I bet you're a dreamer like me. Well, my friend, it's the dreamers like us that change the world! You're still here because you have a fear of failure so strong it won't let you give up, right? However, you probably feel like you've given it all you've got and you just can't figure out what works. I promise it's as simple as doing some work on the inside. It's not easy, but it is simple.

Today, I enjoy spending my mornings with my daughter and son. I'm there when they wake up and I'm present, fully in the moment, grateful for how blessed my life is. My husband and I enjoy life's adventures and our relationship gets stronger and more fulfilling as we better understand each other and ourselves. It's so easy and enjoyable to love and to be loved, when it comes from a place of kindness and understanding.

I love my work. I could do it without getting paid and I'd be happy as ever. I won't, because I love making money, and because I know with more money I can make a bigger impact. I had to get comfortable with the idea that it's not selfish or greedy to be wealthy, a mindset that held me back for years, without my ever knowing it. Does this sound familiar?

My mission will never end, as long as there are women suffering from fear and doubt, falsely believing that they aren't enough, aren't pretty enough, aren't skinny enough or aren't smart enough. I know what it's like to feel like you were meant for more but scared to death that you'd never figure it out. It's hard, and a bit scary, to accept that the key lies within us. Ironically, it is this truth that will set you free. Once you see it working in your life, this truth will set your soul on fire. Once you believe in yourself and your dreams, rest assured that one day they will be your reality.

If you'd like to hear more about my journey and how you can change your thinking, so that you can start living the life you dream about and the life you deserve, visit my website and download my free e-book with more secrets to success.

## Marilynn Reis Sonier

Marilynn Reis Sonier is a success coach, who helps women get out of their own way so that they can start achieving the results they've always wanted in their personal and professional lives. After ten years of entrepreneurial ventures, Marilynn had achieved success but lacked the freedom and fulfillment that she desired. After discovering the secret to success as taught by the master of human potential and wealth building, Bob Proctor, she opened her coaching business to help women deal with the overwhelming prospect of pursuing their professional ambitions, while caring for a family. Today, it is Marilynn's passion to help others get clear on their goals and avoid the common pitfalls that she once faced herself. She enjoys working with individuals and small businesses to define their goals, discover what's holding them back and make the changes that will turn their thinking into results, goals into achievements and dreams into reality. Motivated by her experience as a salon and spa owner, she has merged the science of achievement with financial, marketing, sales and customer service strategies specific to the beauty industry. Her salon mastermind program, Beyond Beauty, combines personal development coaching with a community of salon and spa owners that provides her clients an opportunity to network, strategize and ultimately achieve success, by working on their business instead of in their business. Marilynn is a devoted wife and mother of two residing in Phoenix, Arizona. She is available for speaking engagements, in addition to individual and group coaching.

To learn more about Marilynn, her coaching program Thinking Into Results, or to contact her, visit www.SuccessWithMRS.com.

Marilynn Reis Sonier
Success With MRS
3830 E Kroll Drive
Gilbert, AZ 85234
480-383-9384
Info@SuccessWithMRS.com
www.SuccessWithMRS.com

# Eleonor Forte

## *A Time to Shine: Finding Inner Beauty*

As the only daughter of immigrant parents, I grew up with the understanding that higher education is the ticket to a great career and financial stability. My parents were both physicians with many years of formal education and training both in the Philippines and in the United States. They were tireless workers and sacrificed very much for our family.

I was a very serious student in high school, knowing that I was expected to go to college. I attended Indiana University and pursued a degree in finance from their top-notch business school. Upon graduating, I was ready to make my mark in the business world. I worked for the next 12 years, primarily as a financial analyst in the asset management field. I wanted it all — a great career and a big family. I was well on my way, having married my college sweetheart with three small boys in tow. However, by the time I was pregnant with my fourth bundle of joy, I decided to put my career on hold to stay home and raise my children.

Staying home with the boys seemed like it would be much easier than it was. A full day of work complete with meetings, deadlines, and sometimes even traveling was a piece of cake, compared to staying home all day to take care of four young boys. I envied anyone with a "real job" who got a lunch break, could use the bathroom whenever they needed to, could take a sick day and had a 401(k).

I was prepared for the carpools, playdates, activities, and endless driving in the family minivan. That was a part of my daily routine for many years as a stay at home mom. I knew that most of my time and energy would be devoted to those four little boys. What I wasn't prepared for, were the changes in me that resulted from the time at home.

During those years as a young mother, I consistently found that I was always putting myself last. It came with the territory. I was the first one up and the last one to go to bed. I had grocery shopping to do, meals to make, lunches to pack and endless loads of laundry to do.

## Finding Me

As much as I loved being a mom and taking care of everyone else, I found that I wasn't taking care of myself. As strange as it sounds, I felt like I was slowly losing a part of me. I no longer felt beautiful and often questioned how others saw me. I no longer cared about what I wore whenever I left the house. I had no clue what was in style anymore, nor did I care. My hair was either in a ponytail or under a baseball cap or both. After my fourth pregnancy, I probably put on more weight than I'd care to admit. I remember looking at the mirror and saw that I was heavier with each pregnancy.

Interestingly, what I saw on the outside deeply affected how I felt on the inside. I became very accepting of the fact that I was on the bottom of the proverbial totem pole that I forgot how to take care of myself. I didn't like what I saw in the mirror and, more importantly, how I felt inside.

After my mother lost her battle with cancer in 2006, I sank into a deep depression. The grief was so overwhelming, that I found it difficult to function anymore. I knew that I needed to make some immediate changes and start taking care of myself physically, mentally and emotionally. After getting the boys off to school in the morning, I started my daily walk around the neighborhood. Slowly a fifteen-minute walk turned into a 30-minute jog, which eventually turned into an hour-long run. Running became "my thing," which I looked forward to doing five days a week. The more I ran, the less I wanted to run away. Those who knew me in high school would never believe that I ran my first marathon at age 42. I went on to run three more marathons after that.

Eventually, in 2012, I decided to do something just for me and pursue my passion for photography. I used to photograph sports (a lot of it, since all of the boys played several sports at the same time), schools, weddings and other events. After a few years of photographing different genres, I focused entirely on portraiture. I love the creativity that comes with photographing one client at a time. My "a-ha" moment came, when I starting photographing women. I found that no matter what a woman's stage in life, occupation, background, or age, all women seem to share a common thread. We all have an innate desire to look and feel worthy. However, some women don't feel beautiful and, therefore, don't want their pictures taken. Imagine this for a minute, when one day, your children will look for photos of you. What will they find? They will find many photos of them but what about their mom? We have become so good at capturing the big and small events of our children's lives, that we often forget about us.

As a portrait photographer, I've come to realize that most people, especially women, just don't feel comfortable being in front of the camera. It also seems like the older we get, the more we shy away from the camera. Women are undeniably hard and critical of themselves.

Why is it that we tend to avoid the camera at all? Why do we focus on those problem areas of our faces and bodies that no one else sees? Why can't we open our eyes to see how beautiful we are as individual people? Each of us is special and unique. When did our vision of ourselves become warped and perhaps tied to what we see on social media? Since "beauty is in the eye of the beholder," do we see ourselves differently than how others see us? When I look through my lens and see you at the other end, I can capture something magical that you often don't see, just by looking in the mirror.

I decided that enough was enough. I didn't want to be invisible. I wanted to exist in photos. I wanted my boys to have photos of me and to pass them on to their kids, long after I am gone. As much as I love taking pictures of everyone else, I wanted to hand off my camera to my husband or to a friend to take pictures of me. However, I needed to get over my insecurities about how I looked. Why is it that when I see a picture of myself, all I can see is how bloated I look, how big my arms are, or how short my legs look? Why couldn't I understand that to my family, I look imperfectly perfect? Isn't that how it should be? Inside that imperfectly perfect woman is an inner beauty that radiates from the deep love she feels for her family. She is a loving and caring soul.

As a portrait photographer, I've worked with many women who have felt the same insecurities. Before their photoshoot, I coach them on what to wear, what colors compliment them best, as well as the style of clothing that would look best on them. Posing is one of the most overlooked factors in ensuring that women look fabulous in photos. Often a simple tweak in posing will make a huge difference. When my clients see their portraits, they are amazed and feel very happy about what they see. It is wonderful when a woman loves what she sees and reconnects to that inner belief that she is truly beautiful. When a woman sees herself as beautiful, she experiences a reawakening of her strengths and abilities that manifests itself in a renewed self-confidence. She will project this self-confidence in her work, family life and romantic life.

If you're like most women, you've probably felt one or more of the following:

I'm just not photogenic.

I hate the way that I look in pictures.

I need to lose some weight, before I get my picture taken.

Do you believe that beauty is skin deep or that your true beauty comes from within? There is so much beauty in loving yourself and all that you bring to this world. There is beauty in how you care for your loved ones, your family and your friends. There is beauty in how you help others with all of your God-given gifts and talents.

The truth is that your loved ones think you are perfect the way you are. You should capture who you are at this very moment in a special portrait for you and your loved ones to treasure forever. It will become a meaningful heirloom that can be passed on to future generations. Printed portraits will stand the test of time.

## Showing Beautiful

Not too long ago, I turned 50 years old. Truth be told, as the months, weeks and days inched closer to my birthday, I was dreading it. The "Big 5-0" seemed like a hard birthday to swallow. After all, that is half a century! The big day came and went, as I celebrated with my family and closest friends. And you know what? I didn't feel any different than I did when I was 49. Yet, a couple of years later, I realized that I've changed. No longer do I care about what other people think of me. I'm perfectly content with who I am and where I am in life. I was blessed with an amazing family and will be forever grateful for being able to stay home and raise my boys. I miss those days when they were little, especially since my empty nest is just around the corner.

I love the fact that I took a risk and followed my heart to start my own business in my 40's. I love the fact that I am making a difference, by helping other women see their own beauty through my lens.

## 50 Over 50

This year I've decided to begin a personal photography project called "50 Over 50". I will photography 50 women over the age of 50. I want to capture the inner beauty, strength, wisdom and confidence of women in their 50's, 60's, 70's and beyond. I want to hear their stories of how their definition of beauty has evolved after turning 50. I want to know how their journeys in life have transformed them into the amazing women that they've become. Through this project, I want to show the world that beauty doesn't diminish with age but rather shines brighter than it ever has in these women's lives.

Although this project focuses on women over 50 years old, I love photographing women of all ages at different stages in life. I believe that all women are beautiful without exception! My goal is to photograph as many women as I can, so that I can show them how others see them…beautiful.

If you are over 50 years old and would like more information about my "50 Over 50" project, I invite you to my website for more details.

www.ellefortephotography.com/50-over-50/

After so many years of feeling like I wasn't enough, I love having portraits of myself that have enabled me to reconnect with a part of me that I've lost. I know that after having four children, my body will never be the same as in my early 20's. Every wrinkle, every gray hair and every stretch mark is a gift. What matters more to me is that I love how I feel on the inside. We all have an inner beauty … it just needs a moment to shine.

# Eleonor Forte

Eleonor Forte is a boutique portrait photographer located in the northwest suburbs of Chicago, IL. Her friends call her "Elle," hence the name of her studio, Elle Forte Photography.

Eleonor studied finance at Indiana University and received an MBA in marketing from DePaul University. She worked for 12 years in the corporate world as a financial analyst. Although she enjoyed her job, she longed for something more. Her entrepreneurial business mind eventually merged with her creative spirit and love of photography, which led her to her ultimate career. Her favorite quote is from George Eliot: "It is never too late to be what you might have been."

In April 2020, Eleonor became a Certified Professional Photographer (CPP) for her artistic and technical competence as awarded by the Professional

Photographers of America (PPA). PPA currently recognizes fewer than 2,500 CPPs. Just as doctors and other professionals seek certification in their industries, Eleonor strives to continually master her craft to be the best photographer for her clients.

Eleonor loves to empower women, by helping them look and feel their best through her photography. She aims to bring out the inner beauty, poise and confidence that exist in all women.

Married to her college sweetheart for 26 years, Eleonor is also a dedicated mom of four boys. She loves coffee, wine, and chocolate, although not necessarily in that order. She is a romantic at heart and will cry about almost anything that touches her heart.

Eleonor Forte, CPP
Elle Forte Photography
2200 Stonington Avenue, Suite 100
Hoffman Estates, IL 60169
847-502-2002
Info@ElleFortePhotography.com
www.ElleFortePhotography.com

# Ericka Axtle-Ludwig

## *Turning Black Ice Into Diamonds*

Hands in pockets, looking down at my frozen feet in my one good pair of shoes, once pristine shiny black heels now caked in salt and dirty ice from wintry Pennsylvanian streets, I told myself, *just two more blocks, you're almost there.*

Leaving my first husband wasn't easy.

Moving to the U.S.A. from Mexico City with my first husband was a culture shock, but I embraced the adventure with an open heart. Gripping the handle of my one suitcase, arriving in Pennsylvania in the summer of 1998, I immediately fell in love with the gorgeous, bushy trees, with birds singing from their perches. Growing up in a strict Mexican Catholic family meant women did not live with their boyfriends, until they became their husbands. As a result, I couldn't see his secret life of substance abuse and came to realize that my decision to escape an overprotective father and machismo society clouded my judgment. When the lies started, emotional and verbal abuse was quick to follow. In my heart, I knew it was over. However, with no job, no friends (yet!), no car and no license (I was almost 4,000 miles from home), I was stranded. On top of everything, my grandmother, "Abuelita" and mentor passed away two days before Christmas.

It was one of the most emotionally challenging times of my life as an adult. However, I believe that you have to be your own motivation and your own love to step into your power that only you possess. I know there's a little voice in every single one of us, sparking deeply within our hearts and it wants to be unstoppable.

*I* wanted to be unstoppable. Little did I know, I was one long walk in the snow away from having it all.

*Back to my frozen feet.* I bent over to rub my pinky toe back to life, arriving in the heated historic hotel lobby, snowflakes melting in my hair. This was it, my very first interview in the U.S.A., and I nailed it! That momentum was so empowering. I was no longer finding my way. I was on my way!

Working the front desk meant that I would have my own money and my own freedom. First were AAA driving courses, then my dream car and finally my divorce. My bilingual skills in hospitality led to my next opportunity as a translator for a newly relocated Spanish manufacturing company. This would open the most important door of all, leading me to my true love, my second husband. In 2003, we built our loving home in the Pennsylvanian countryside. Since I grew up in a city with many buildings and lots of hustle and bustle, our peaceful home in the woods has filled my animal-loving heart with great joy. In 2005, we welcomed our daughter into the world. Life was glorious, and about to be seriously shaken up by a patch of black ice, a birthday cake and a silver Mitsubishi Eclipse.

*"There is no force equal to a woman determined to rise."*
— W.E.B Dubois

In high school, a group of girls bullied me. Each day a brand new torture of dirt mixed into my makeup, gum in my hair and there were slaps, punches and name-calling. Sitting with my back against the cafeteria wall, I'd quickly eat my strategically packed salad, ready to attack with my fork. As a competitive gymnast, I was strong. However, being part of the ugliness wasn't me. I was the girl who dotted her "I's" with hearts, and still do.

*Own your magic.*

As the bullying became more violent, I started weightlifting. I figured if I looked like Wonder Woman, they'd leave me alone! My body felt good, and my sporty guy friends made me feel safe. While the weight room had my back, my grandmother helped me control my mind, pushing me to see I was strong and capable beyond deadlifts. On low days, Abuelita would jump on my bed beside me and say, "Oh yes, you can!" and "The demons in your head are garbage, so put them in the trash where they belong!". She'd tell me to have a powerful mindset and would write me notes of encouragement, which I still call on for strength to this day, decades later.

When I tell people my high school stories, they nod their heads. They say that they can picture the scene straight out of an American high school movie, without realizing I grew up in Mexico City. My home was rich in culture, and our food was full of flavor. Each dish was crafted from old recipe books passed down through generations of women, great grandmother to Abuelita to my mother, and finally to me. There were machismo men with agendas and strong women doing the best they could to raise families while working. My mother and father propelled me forward and encouraged me to live out in the world. However, they were quick to remind me of my roots. I am grateful for those lessons and my family's love. As an ethnic Mexican, I proudly wear my accent. However, the rules and expectations for women are strict (especially during the 1970s and 80s). The persistent violence saddens me, which is why we must go forward.

> *"Just when the caterpillar thought the world*
> *was over, it became a butterfly."*
>
> — Chuang Tzu

In early February 2006, I visited our local bakery to pick up my daughter's first birthday cake and show her off a little, the way new moms do. It was a big blue sky kind of day, with a few patches of snow on the ground. Placing her cake gently down next to her, I buckled her car seat, kissed her cheek and revved up our silver, turbocharged Mitsubishi Eclipse, my dream car, as we slipped out of the parking spot. A truly remarkable day, perfect for black ice.

Peaceful and serene one moment, our white-knuckled fight for our lives came out of nowhere, as our car spun out of control. Everything slowed down. I saw flashes of my life — Abuelita, my fairytale wedding in a Scottish Castle, holding my daughter in my arms — then I saw the brick church.

I knew if I didn't do something, we'd hit on my daughter's side. Gripping the steering wheel with all of my strength, I willed our car to spin around to my side, the left side, pleading with my mind and pulling with all of my weight. As the first brick pillar of the church entrance sign exploded around us, pain shot up my left side, crushing my two-door dream car into a half-moon nightmare, my driver's side seat covered in brick and glass, my door pinning me in place. I craned my neck and stretched to look for my daughter. Anxiety started to creep in, but the second I heard her cry, relief washed over me. I was very thankful that she was alive and help was on the way.

*Expect Miracles.*

Remarkably, nothing happened to my daughter that day. However, a change occurred within me. We planted a wisteria vine in our yard in honor of our daughter, which we still marvel at to this day. A beautiful butterfly garden, a frog and fish pond, majestic trees, and tender care transformed the old farmer's field into a living, breathing testament of our love for each other.

There's an old saying, "If you go looking for trouble, you'll find it." The same goes for goodness and motivation. I started looking for it everywhere, my eyes open to it, my heart seeking it out and the gym was no exception. Being a gym lover, I hooked up with a transformation coach. She would send me motivational sayings, reminding me of all those years ago when my grandmother would encourage me. I even went a step further. I became a certified personal trainer and started gathering and creating my own quotes.

The simplest thing you can do is raise another woman up, like my grandmother did with me (now my mission and inspiration). Encourage her and give her positive feedback, so she can grow and learn to use her unique voice to change the world. All it takes is hearing something simple yet powerful: "You got this!" "Yes, You Can" "Believe In You" "You're Enough" "You're Freaking Unstoppable"!

**Being An Entrepreneur Is For The Brave**

Being a mom was my engine powering me through life, since I always wanted a strong daughter. Now, 15 years later, I can honestly say that she is my heart and soul, strength personified, Unstoppable Girl Power in the flesh! She is a 2nd degree Black Belt in Taekwondo, a talented violinist, dedicated to her studies and passions in life, ultra-smart, kind and capable of taking on the world. Teaching gentleness with resilience and softness paired with grit is always a focus. Becoming a mom shook me to my core and truly prepared me to be an entrepreneur, both with daily challenges that I wholeheartedly embrace. My motivational words, which would become my flagship product, started with post-it notes I'd leave for my daughter anywhere she would see them.

... you're strong.

... you're brave.

... you're beautiful.

... you're unstoppable!

"100 Ways to Empower Your Child" came out of that. Then inspirational decals, wallpaper series and products. Long before my entrepreneurial skills fully emerged, I knew my calling was to inspire women like me, who wished they had been empowered earlier in life, and young ladies, like my daughter. I wanted to help them step into their power, boost their confidence to lift their voice and ultimately send their message out into the world with my "Girl Power 24/7" motivational product lines.

*Make each day your masterpiece.*

Being unstoppable doesn't mean I don't struggle or suffer at times. As an entrepreneur, there are many lonely days, late nights and disagreements with manufacturers (since I deal with physical products made in the U.S.A.). At the same time, I am also raising my daughter and nurturing my marriage. As this is written, we're all in the grip of a (highly) politicized pandemic, a time when we need extra motivation and inspiration more than ever.

Surrounding myself with motivational words, supportive friends and family, and doing what I can daily to get even a tiny step closer to my end goal, keeps me grounded. I firmly believe in going toward my happiness, while making a positive impact on the world and women's lives. My newest Girl Power Motivational Wallpaper has my favorite mantra of all time, *don't stop until you're proud.* I look at it every day and try to do at least one thing to make my family, myself and my clients proud.

## Get GLOWING & Exist LOUDLY!

What is an unstoppable woman? She rises from within, even on the days she wants to curl up in bed. She masters her thoughts but knows when to reach out for help. She is me, and she is you. She lives inside every woman. When you silence the self-doubt, you decide not to give away your power you have possessed and stop dimming your light. She is radiant and able to raise the bar for herself, leading by example for others.

Every woman has unique gifts, talents, skills and abilities. No one else can show up as she can to make her own impact in the world.

You will succeed, when you trust yourself. I know you can look at your past circumstances and think you are stuck, but your past doesn't define your true potential. You decide to pick up those pieces, to extract the lessons and the nuggets of wisdom to reclaim your power. Honor the woman you are aspiring to be and the woman you are right now in this world to fulfill your purpose. I want you to come from a grateful heart, step into your power and really own who you are. My challenge for you is to look in the mirror and tell yourself that you're unstoppable! Ask yourself, "How am I making a difference?" Then go out and make it happen!

You can become the "you" of your dreams. Because all you need is already inside of you.

## Ericka Axtle-Ludwig

Ericka Axtle-Ludwig believes in magic, specifically, the magic in each and every one of us. In January 2010, she became a U.S. citizen and by 2011 she created her first corporation, setting the base of her entrepreneurial journey.

She is an NCSF Certified Personal Trainer, a TRX Personal Trainer and holds a Bachelor's Degree in Communication Science as well as an English Teacher Certification. She is currently impacting lives as Owner and Chief Graphic Designer of Motivational Wall Decor, building her brand, Girl Power 24/7, soon to include even more dynamic Women's Motivational products.

Her passion and personal self-motivation is to empower women with her Girl Power Wallpaper Series, Motivational Quotes and Affirmation Decals, and Sweat In Style Fitness Apparel which has impacted lives around the world. Some of her clients have turned drab bathrooms into POWERrooms, dominating their mornings with affirmation filled pep talks and can-do attitudes or even boosted blah office spaces into Institutions of Inspiration. Her devoted fans adorn their small businesses, beauty salons and home offices with beautifully designed, powerfully uplifting words to Make An IMPACT!

Her advice, products, insights and artwork have been featured in pop-up shops around Pennsylvania for Breast Cancer Awareness and Advocacy and across the internet through major publications, such as Oxygen Magazine Challenge Groups (#oxysisters!) as well as STRONG magazine elite fitness squad social media groups. She provides inspirational fitness trackers, refrigerator inspiration and all things motivational fitness for women worldwide through her omnichannel social media presence. She is always working on her communications to better serve women in need of motivation. Be sure to check out any of her numerous 5-star-rated Amazon reviews of her Girl Power Wallpaper Series or make your own miracles happen at: www.GirlPower247. com.

Ericka Axtle-Ludwig
Girl Power 24/7
632 Whisler Road
Etters, PA 17319
717-932-5914
Ericka@GirlPower247.com
www.GirlPower247.com

# Maren Oslac

## *Dancing with Life*

Change how you see the world, and the world will change.

We all have defining moments in our lives. Moments of choice where we know we will never be the same. My world radically changed on November 6, 2019, in one moment of choice.

I had just completed a 10-day pilgrimage through India, Nepal, and Tibet: a life-altering trip, with a surprise ending. That surprise ending was the moment I got to choose an entirely new future.

I was on my way home. I felt infinitely closer to the divine from my trip, plus I had scored a first-class seat for the international flight! Life was good.

And Spirit has a sense of humor.

I landed in Beijing to change planes and go through customs, at which point security detained me, told me my Visa was not valid, that I was in their country illegally, and that I would not be allowed to leave until I resolved the issue.

I had $20 worth of Chinese Yuan, a cell phone that only worked on WiFi, and I didn't speak a word of Chinese. The police escorted me out of the airport with a single clue: an address for Visa Services in downtown Beijing, written in Chinese, on a small scrap of paper.

Holy SHIT!

Interestingly, my life had not only led to, but prepared me for, that very moment.

## Becoming a Leader

I came into the world with a strong drive and a mind of my own. My mother barely went into labor, and, poof, I was here. I was ready. Bring on life!

In my youth, I was sure I was born to be an elite swimmer, a champion. Born in June, I was swimming that very summer. The water was my first love.

It turns out that inspiring people was also an early calling. My older brother, who had shunned the water, saw me in the pool as a baby and decided that it was time to jump in. The next year, we were both in swim lessons, which led to a local swim club and swimming as a passion.

I started life in Pennsylvania, and I'm not sure if it's the simplicity of youth, or if life really was that magical; I recall it as pure joy, an idyllic period of innocence, connection, and freedom. When I was seven, we moved to Chicago, and my pure, open, and joyful life began to change. Our extended family lived in the Chicago area, which was mostly exciting, and it came with some definite life lessons.

My paternal grandfather (Poppy to us grandkids) was a larger than life figure, volatile and opinionated, with tight control over his family. And my experience as a young girl was that Poppy had no use for me.

In his world, women and children were to be seen and not heard. I was both. He treated me differently from the other three grandkids (boys), and I didn't understand why. To me, we were the same. I looked like them (short-cropped hair), I played like them (refused to wear dresses to my mom's chagrin) and did everything they did (sports, loved Tonka trucks, etc.) Most people mistook me for a boy.

My grandfather, however, did not, and excluded me from his 'boys' club.

He would take the three boys places, give them things, and leave me out. My parents would console me and try to make it up to me, which just solidified the feeling that somehow I wasn't good enough.

One example: Poppy loved betting on the horses and went to the track every week, often taking the boys with him. Occasionally, dad went and allowed me to tag along. Before each race, my grandfather would coach the boys on the horses, hand them a few small bills send them off to place bets. Yes, I was excluded.

Poppy's views didn't sit right with my older brother. Anytime he got something I didn't, he would find a way to share it with me. At the track, he'd find me, share what he'd learned (and the money), and we'd go place our bets together.

While I was learning a deep shame around being female from my grandfather, my 10-year-old brother was handing me a lifeline. His pure conviction that I was worthwhile, and the enormous capacity of his heart, kept a door open inside of me that might have otherwise slammed shut.

*Grace comes wrapped in unexpected packages.*

Layers were forming. My grandfather dismissed me based on gender. I then watched my father build an empire, transforming himself from a poor grad student into an influential, powerful, and wealthy businessman. The stage was set for me to embrace society's sexist beliefs and follow the path of so many women just like me. I claimed the dominant, masculine qualities within while quietly locking away my misunderstood feminine power.

I was a driven soul. I came in with a purpose, and the path to success seemed evident to my young self. I went all-in and spent decades studying goal setting, success principles, frameworks, and making things happen. I simultaneously dismissed and diminished my feminine side.

Luckily for me, I did have a balancing force in my life: mom. She introduced me to spirituality and a path of self-actualization before I was ten. I had found my second love of this lifetime.

## Hiding My Light

My first love, swimming, was still going strong. It was the one place where everything fell away. My parents' separation, my grandfather's ignorance, all issues big and small, none of it mattered. Swimming was my refuge. I was happiest in the pool, head down and in my zone. I'd show up early to practices, put in 110%, and leave energized. I was setting records and moving up the ranks season after season. In junior high, I caught the attention of an Olympic coach who invited me to work with him. I was SO excited.

The hammer fell. My parents said no.

Training to be an Olympian would require exceptional dedication. I was ready and willing. My parents wanted me to have a 'normal' childhood: friends, school, parties, etc.

I was devastated. I wanted exceptional.

My swimming started to deteriorate after that. I'd taken on my parent's desire for me, throttling back my drive and squashing my passion. I swam on my high school and college teams, but it wasn't the same; the gold medal champion was gone. I'd chosen to douse my inner fire instead of doubling down and taking a different route to my dream.

That choice impacted the next 30 years of my life and led to my current work: helping people connect to, and live, their deep passions.

The process of reclaiming the longing of my youth also led directly to that moment in Beijing in 2019. Spirit's hand was at work. If I had not been 'derailed' in achieving my Olympic dream, I would never have found my third love of this lifetime, couples dance.

**Surrender and the Conversation**

In my twenties, I had figured out the success game and was rocking it! I was an up-and-coming, top commercial photographer in a completely male-dominated field. I landed a job as one of only four photographers on a big shoot in Oklahoma City.

For a week, we put in long days of shooting, followed by evenings out at a local country bar. Wham. My first exposure to couples dancing. I had found my third love; I just didn't know it yet. Back in Chicago, my friends refused to explore Country couples dancing, so I looked up the local country bar and went by myself.

I don't do anything halfway. I devoured lessons at the bar and found my way to the nearby Ballroom studio. I started competing (absolutely terrified, and entirely determined). I said yes to every opportunity.

I had a goal: to be able to follow anyone doing any dance. I wanted to be the best follower ever. I know, small goal, right?

Following requires a unique skill set, which is not the same set needed to win competitions. Competitions are about learning choreography, knowing your steps, and executing — straight forward, linear, predictable, and very much in line with the successful 'Maren' I'd cultivated.

Following is a skill of entering the unknown and waiting there, fully present, in poise, ready to respond. Imagine a cat stalking a mouse. She is still and wholly present. She builds life force, prepared to pounce, not orchestrating, or trying to make things happen. She's not 'figuring out' how to get the mouse to come out, tear down the wall, or impose her will. She is surrendered and in the moment.

This ability was foreign and outside of my realm of experience, and it was calling me. Compelled to master it, my high-rational-achiever-self got to work and did just that. I now call it "active surrender," the art of being fully engaged in the conversation, while not anticipating or planning what to say next.

Active surrender is the skill that sought me, a skill with a fighting chance to emerge thanks to the conviction of a 10-year-old, a skill that is a lost art and completely undervalued - the heart of the feminine and, sadly, dismissed by society.

**Dance as a Metaphor for Life**

My outer journey, learning to become a masterful follower, reflected inward, waking the feminine that I had demeaned and dismissed for so many years. I was ignorant, and she patiently waited and allowed me to find her, as is her way.

She showed me her value; the empowerment of owning the other side of the coin. I began surrendering to life instead of continually pushing through it.

I applied my active surrender skills

- to my relationships, and found my future husband so quickly that I wasn't ready when he asked me to marry him

- to my business, and manifested a coach in Bali, plus the money to cover the trip and his ongoing business mastermind program, to take me to the next level of my business

- to my Dancing With Life Movement and opportunities opened like a flood gate in front of me, leading me clearly from one to the next

**Full Circle**

And I manifested myself detained in Beijing.

After two hours of interrogation by Chinese officials, I was escorted by police out of the secure section of the airport and left there with my one clue; the small slip of paper with the Beijing address.

I spent an hour just trying to track down my luggage. With no bags in sight, and a man yelling at me in Chinese, I was about to break down. I stopped in my tracks and knew I had a choice. It was my moment, THAT moment.

I saw two clear options. I could power through, get angry, be upset, and continue applying logic to an illogical situation. (Two hours of logic had already proved futile with the customs officers).

> "The definition of insanity is doing the same thing over and
> over again and expecting different results."
> — Albert Einstein

Or, I could take the road less traveled: active surrender. I could put knowledge into practice, something I'd already done with my dance partner, my life partner, and my businesses. I had a chance to do it now. To show up, fully present in the conversation with Spirit, and trust that She had my back.

I did. And She did.

*The way I got out of China was full, active surrender - all my learning culminating in that one moment.*

I didn't just 'get out,' either. I spent four extraordinary days in China, and I was thoroughly taken care of the entire time. Amazing people emerged to help me, hotel rooms, transportation, and food appeared. I had everything I needed and then some. Spirit's timing was flawless, and she perfectly orchestrated every detail without me figuring out one piece.

My whole life led to that moment of self-determination. I changed how I saw my life, and my life changed. The magic that happened was beyond anything that I could have created.

Because of that moment, I've doubled down on my mission to help others who feel this truth deep in their bones but can't quite articulate it. My transformative process shifts their 'inarticulate knowing' into tangible, practical guidance in everyday life.

I passionately believe that the magic of life is not limited to a select few; it is everyone's birthright. My step by step micro book, *The Ultimate Guide to Life Spinning in Your Favor*, is free and downloadable from my website (MarenOslac.com).

If you are inspired, I'd love to hear your story and invite you to add your voice to our Dancing with Life private Facebook group.

**Maren Oslac**

Maren is the Founder and Chief Education Officer at Heart & Sole Dance, a transformational ballroom studio outside of Chicago. She is also a business disrupter transforming the old school 'push-your-way-through-to-get-ahead' business paradigm to one of flow and grace using the fundamental concepts of couples dancing.

Maren's triple career as a champion dancer, preeminent educator and serial entrepreneur coalesced into "Dance With Life,"; a one-of-kind program that breaks the "efforting-for-success trap" that influential leaders struggle to escape.

After years of striving and pushing to attain success, Maren bridged the gap between her spiritual life and business life to connect to a place of deep listening and limitless flow. This resulted in greater success than striving ever produced, accompanied by inner peace and congruence.

Whether in her studio or working with successful business owners, Maren is committed to helping people create a deeper, richer conversation with life. She empowers them to play a bigger game, step into their true calling and dance their most authentic dance - abundantly, joyfully and inflow.

Maren revels in sharing this approach with fellow travelers who know like she did, "that there is a better way." Visit her website to download *The Ultimate Guide to Life Spinning in Your Favor* to tap into the guidance and endless abundance that is your birthright.

Maren Oslac
Heart & Sole Dance
Joliet, IL 60433
MarenDance@hotmail.com
www.MarenOslac.com
www.HeartSoleDance.com

# Tiffany N. Lewis

## *Working Motherhood Is Not for the Faint Hearted*

If you're a wildly ambitious woman, then you know how the right shade of lipstick paired with a dream can have you feeling like you're going to change the world.

*I felt unstoppable.*

I had just made it through a difficult divorce, and I had a different outlook on life. All the hard work that I had invested in my marketing career was finally taking me to new heights. I made great money, was challenged daily, traveled often and was deep into developing marketing strategies proven to produce. I was on fire for an industry I loved, but I always felt like something was missing.

Looking back, this was one of those perception vs. reality dilemmas that many of us face. I was climbing the mountain to success. However, when I got there, I felt the weight of corporate politics and a sense of isolation, as I exchanged once accepted invitations for fun for long nights of mounting work. At a crossroads, I asked myself, *"Is this the life I want, that I had worked so hard for?"*

I decided to start dating seriously again and ended up marrying a long-time friend from high school. It's kind of funny how things work out, but he let me be me. I did not have to take a step back from ambition and independence for my relationship. He didn't ask me to sacrifice, like I had been expected to sacrifice before. This relationship was different, and I also started looking at my future in a different light.

If you had asked me before my late 20s if I wanted children, you would have most certainly been met with a "hell no." I LOVED my nieces more than anything, and I vowed to be the best aunt in the world. However, I was not sure that I could see myself being a mother. I honestly viewed myself as pretty selfish in the pursuit of the life I wanted to live — one of "get-up-and-go" and spending my money fulfilling my biggest dreams!

Knowing this, it should come as no surprise that before I became a mom, I was confident that I would continue traveling at the same pace, living life at the same pace (missing zero experiences and opportunities for self-care) and working at the same pace. Feel free to enjoy a laugh at my expense, if you know where this is going.

*...what I did not know was how much I would love that little five-pound, nine-ounce baby when she arrived.*

In waltzed little Mallory Lynn in the early hours of a Wednesday morning, and at the risk of sounding cliché, I KNEW life was never going to be the same. She had a head full of beautiful black hair, and she had the biggest eyes I had ever seen on someone so small. All that talk about not missing a beat with my career quickly turned to, "I would live in a cardboard box to avoid going back to my job in corporate America." I could find happiness in a cardboard box, as long as I still had my baby, right? My husband would find a way instead of a reason to keep loving me, wouldn't he? *Shit.*

*Reflecting on these early moments, makes my heart skip a beat. It simultaneously makes me want to put my foot in my mouth for all of the things I said "I thought" motherhood would be to other mothers. Consider this to be my very overdue apology.*

Over the next few months, we battled a milk allergy, colic, reflux and our first bout of RSV. I can now admit that I had some serious post-postpartum depression and anxiety. With all of that looming, the pressure also mounted to return to work. I felt completely devastated. I now knew how stay-at-home moms became stay-at-home moms. However, I still had that spark for marketing, and I didn't want to lose it. Sure, I thought about looking for a less demanding job, I thought about monetizing an invention (which I did partly pursue), and, of course, a remote position would be ideal!

*P.S. anyone who has the time to jump jobs after maternity leave is a goddess in my book. If I had spare time, I was choosing a shower — (without the baby in the bassinet outside of the door, all the while hearing phantom cries).*

Long story short, I returned to work part-time, commuting at least two hours per day to a global marketing job in a technical field, while my daughter went to daycare. Maybe it was my naivety as a first-time mom, but I did not know to expect the amount of sickness that would follow. It seemed like one to two times per month, my husband and I were juggling our jobs trying to care for our baby with minimal outside help. When our daughter was sick, she wanted momma, and I wanted to be there for her. This naturally created a mom/work/life imbalance.

I traveled a fair amount the first year, but it wasn't the same. It wasn't fun, mysterious, or thrilling to be in different parts of the country, while my baby was without me. Every time I stepped onto that plane, my heart escaped my body for a brief moment, and several moments thereafter. The worry filled me from head-to-toe. I was full of "what-ifs." I genuinely wondered every day, if I was making the right decision.

I longed for a job closer to home without travel. I simultaneously found myself daydreaming about starting my own digital marketing business to get back to the light-hearted pieces of marketing, so I pursued both. A friend of mine referred me for an open position with a new company, and in the interim, I pursued "More Meaningful Marketing" — a digital marketing company that could knock it out of the park on creating an authentic content marketing experience with personal branding at its core.

The new company prided itself on work/life balance and experiencing an upward growth trajectory. I applied and got an interview. It felt right.

On my way to the interview, I thought, "If I'm going to find a better balance as a working mom, I have to be fully transparent." Therefore, when one of the department executives asked my biggest strength, I answered honestly: *"I will put in rock star work every day while I'm here and I will often work through lunches. Becoming a mother has made me a more efficient and dedicated employee. However, at the end of the day, my goal is to spend more time with my daughter."*

We also talked openly about how often my daughter was getting sick to ensure the flexibility was there when needed. I felt excited, bold and nervous, all at the same time. Everything was on the table. The best part was, I got the job!

*I was back to feeling unstoppable. They say success isn't linear, right? Wait, who is "they" anyway?*

I hit the ground running in my new role. My boss was amazing, and she loved to empower other women. Our team was supportive, innovative and firing on all cylinders, without missing a beat. We were getting complimented on the projects we were working on, and I felt much better about the balance I was able to strike between my personal and professional life.

In my spare time, I worked on my side hustle to get to back to the more light-hearted parts of marketing — creating on-target messaging with storytelling at the center. I wanted it to be my only hustle. I wanted to achieve this "life-by-design" that people talked about as a sort of unattainable mythological creature. I knew one thing. If I were going to accomplish any type of mythological creature status, it would most certainly be a Phoenix — rising from the ashes. How appropriate that is, when I think about it in hindsight.

While I had a better balance, my daughter was still often sick, which made this balancing act nearly impossible. My boss had been amazingly supportive, though I could tell it put her in a tough spot at times. She spoke highly of me, my work ethic and my marketing experience. It was a breath of fresh air when it seemed at times like I was making it on prayers, fumes and an unhealthy amount of caffeine. After six months, I found out that she was leaving the company.

At this point, I was working from home a couple of times per month, and it simply wasn't socially acceptable. To make matters more challenging, I was getting a new boss. I tried to embrace the change with open arms, but I had that feeling in the pit of my stomach upon meeting her, that things weren't going to be okay for me.

As I'm sitting here thinking about how to share the next part of my story with you, my first thoughts are how much vulnerability it takes to share a story like mine (although I preach it all the time in my business, it's really not easy for me), and simultaneously how tragically common our experiences can be as working mothers.

Three months in, my new boss was making things hard for me. She belittled me, gave me a lot of her work and treated me like I was beneath her. She seemed to have very little positive or constructive feedback, which was extremely discouraging. My boss was a woman with two small children, which I think disappoints me the most. I know that not all women empower other women. However, we can do so much when we are united! I was hoping for some empathy and understanding. Instead, I was met with unrealistic expectations, and I felt set up to fail under her management.

I looked at my work and personal lives together with an objective eye. I thought to myself, "maybe I am falling behind. I am awfully distracted with how sick my daughter has been." I reviewed my job description, documented my accomplishments and looked for places where I could improve.

I felt guilty every step of the way. You know that "mom guilt" thing? It followed me everywhere. I felt guilty for switching jobs for what I thought would be a better change for my family. Instead, it brought about chaos, trying to balance it all. I felt guilty for not being there for my daughter as much as she needed me. I felt guilty for letting work win, and I felt guilty for letting life win. There was no in-between.

While preparing for my upcoming review, I confided in HR when asked if everything was going alright. In hindsight, I wish I had said, "no," but I didn't. I expressed that I felt very misled having left a job where I was established, to be in such a seemingly downward spiral.

I felt like I was doing whatever it took. I worked through most lunches. My mother, who worked nights, came over immediately after her shift to watch my daughter for the entire day at times, and at other times, until my husband or I could work through lunch or accumulate enough PTO to relieve her. I worked odd hours — waking up before my daughter to get online, and working again when she was in bed. I was determined to make this job work.

I asked for our talk to be kept confidential until after my review, some other big projects were wrapped up and our annual conference was completed. I felt like these would be great ways to prove myself. To be honest, I loved the impact I was able to make in such a short time. It kept me energized.

I was feeling torn at every seam. My daughter often needed me, and I suffered so much mental anguish sending a half-sick child to daycare, that I could hardly stand it — calling during breaks just to make sure she was hanging in there. "They" say "having children is like having your heart living outside of your body." *Wait, who are "they" again?!*

Somehow, in the chain of command, my boss was told about this conversation. To say I was blindsided, would be an understatement. My boss pulled me into her office with an exaggerated account of what I had said and berated me. I was humiliated. I pondered if it was unprofessional to have even said anything at all. I was mortified, and the relationship only got worse from there.

Well, they let me finish working until all of those projects I mentioned earlier were completed, then they fired me. They FIRED me, which still upsets me as I reveal it once again. However, guess what? It turned my life upside down in ALL the best ways, so I'm not going to burden you with the details of how I sat in a dark hole for a little bit of time, feeling sorry for myself, eating WAY too much ice cream...

*I'll tell you how I kept going. How I persevered. How I made lemons out of lemonade — with vodka, shaken, not stirred, on the rocks, please.*

You know that passion project I told you about earlier? The one I started to get back to the fun parts of marketing? I decided to pursue it with all my heart, and this was my chance. I knew I wanted to be with my daughter more, which was the way to do it. You know that quote that says, *"I'd rather work 80 hours a week for myself than 40 for someone else?"* Well, I went all-in on my dream, and I choose it every single day.

What started as taking a couple of jobs here and there grew into a *"holy shit, I need to hire some help"* kind of thing. Talk about a working mom's dream come true! My side hustle became my only hustle.

I don't want to glamorize the climb, because it came with plenty of bumps and bruises. I know we can all be guilty of comparing someone's ending to our middle. I'm here to tell you that if you want something badly enough, you can have it, too. If you think a "life-by-design" is a fallacy, I'm here to tell you it's possible, if you want it enough. I have balance in motherhood as the best reason to want it enough.

What is your reason? Your why? Mine is that for many women before us (my mother included), living a life on your terms, while raising a family wasn't within the realm of possibility.

I am watching my daughter grow up. It's happening too quickly for my comfort, but I'm here for it. The early morning snuggles, the small scrapes that require a very decorative and desired bandage, for the tantrums, for the meals we cook and share together. I'M HERE FOR ALL OF IT.

I empathize with working moms because I KNOW how fast it feels like the time goes for you. I empathize with stay-at-home-moms, too, because I KNOW how slowly it feels like the time goes for you.

*I hope that I made you laugh. If it didn't, I apologize. I have been called out on occasion for my dark humor. That is one thing that motherhood hasn't changed.*

Some moms love to be stay-at-home-moms, and I think that is wonderful. However, there are also moms who give up their careers and dreams, due to the financial strain of childcare or because the balance of doing both becomes impossible. I think that is bullshit, and if you're bursting at the seams for something more meaningful in your life or business, don't lose your identity in motherhood. You know what I'm talking about. That nagging feeling that too much time has gone by without doing something for yourself.

Ignore that voice in your head that says, "I'm a mom. I can't have (fill in the blank) anymore. I'm a mom, I have to sacrifice (fill in the blank). I'm a mom, I have to behave like (fill in the blank).

I'm here to tell you, sister. I may be a mom, but I still drop an "F-Bomb" on occasion (then, blame grandma because my super conservative husband still refuses to deem this as acceptable behavior). Welp, now they both know. Sorry not sorry.

I hope you will join me on your own unstoppable journey because you can do it. It's not the end, it's just the beginning for you to create the work and life that you have always imagined. I have a life beyond what I thought was possible. You can have it all, too — with or without a drink on occasion. I won't judge.

To learn more about Tiffany, and how she can help you create unstoppable content for your business, plus to download your free ebook, visit www.moremeaningfulmarketing.com/creating-unstoppable-content.

**Tiffany N. Lewis**

Tiffany N. Lewis of More Meaningful Marketing is a mother and an avid coffee drinker, with a wit and true passion for creating unstoppable content that is proven to produce.

After losing her corporate job for being a mom first, Tiffany vowed to follow her dreams of building a successful digital marketing business, while watching her daughter grow.

Tiffany believes that the story you tell others about your brand becomes the cornerstone of why your clients do business and continue doing business with you. Therefore, she's passionate about merging personal and professional branding to create an authentic, unforgettable marketing experience.

Just when she thinks she's got it all figured out, 90% of the time, she's wondering if she walked out of the house with mismatched shoes, which reminds her that it's important to stay humble.

Tiffany N. Lewis
More Meaningful Marketing
1293 Arndale Road
Stow, OH 44224-2358
330-329-6934
Tiffany@MoreMeaningfulMarketing.com
www.MoreMeaningfulMarketing.com

# Rebecca Wright

## *Alone in a Busy World*

I have always felt alone, even in a group of people or in small personal gatherings with my best of friends. I felt always just outside the inner circle. I felt included, but not connected. That sense of aloneness caused a desperation for connection. Connection to me meant not only being included but also valued, belonging, understood and more importantly, loved.

At an early age, I felt my first lack of connection, when my father chose to stop parenting me. It was then that I first felt alone, while the world carried on around me. My brother continued to have weekend visitation with our father and that relationship carried on seamlessly. I would watch weekend after weekend for years, as my father arrived for my brother and bought him home. It was as if my presence or lack thereof changed nothing for them. That situation shattered my sense of value and belonging. I lost a connection not only to a parent but to a sibling, an entire side of my extended family and ultimately myself. If I didn't belong in my own family, how would I ever belong anywhere else? I no longer felt loved or worthy of love. I felt alone as though the world just kept getting busier around me and for me.

I convinced myself that the sure way to inclusion, connection and never feeing alone, was to never miss out socially, regardless of what was happening, and to work extra hard to excel and stand out professionally. What seemed to come so effortlessly for others, was exhausting for me. It felt as if everyone had someone and something and I became increasingly alone in spaces full of people and activity.

In my twenties, I was living in Chicago, Illinois and then Atlanta, Georgia. These were two places, where busy was a standard of life. I was working in high-intensity law enforcement jobs and socially doing all the things that busy major cities had to offer. In Chicago, it was flag football on the lake, all the professional sporting events and every festival that Chicago has to offer. If are familiar with Chicago, you know there is never a time without some amazing festival. In Atlanta, it meant clubs and dancing, cultural festivals and exploring historical sites. They were all very much a good time and time consuming, but somehow I never felt like I truly fit in or belonged with the people I was doing all those fun things with. They were not my people, but rather just people to be busy with. I was craving deeper conversation, energizing interactions and inspiring outings. I had friends, good friends actually, and I was hardly ever physically alone, but I never obtained that sense of connection. I constantly wondered why none of that came effortlessly to me, as it did for everyone else.

After Atlanta, I found my way to Montana serving with the AmeriCorps. This time, I was prepared not to be surrounded by busy. It was Montana after all. I was, however, hoping to find like-minded people who were also dedicating their time to volunteering, serving and giving back. I did, in fact, meet an amazing human being that I am certain is a soul mate friendship. However, since I couldn't let go of old habits and was desperate for connection, I also fell in love with a narcissist who certainly felt he had hit the jackpot of desperation in meeting me. This absolutely left me feeling not only alone but completely isolated from all that I was hoping for in Montana. Despite several years in that relationship, I was fortunate enough to get out and far away. This time, I moved to Phoenix, Arizona.

All of the moves I made were done in search of effortless, feel good, connections. The distance and new places made the feeling of being alone in a busy world somehow acceptable because time would be needed to find my place in these new locations. Each move put thousands of miles between circumstances, where I felt as if I had failed to find connections and hope for opportunities to find meaningful and fulfilling connections.

Here I was, in my thirties, unmarried, with no children and yet another new career. Personal relationships, old and new, became challenging, since I was unable to connect with friends, who were now busy with marriage and parenthood. They were all things the busy world was serving up for others and somehow always missing me.

It was after a particularly isolating children's birthday party, that I realized my desperation to become connected was the exact reason I was always finding myself more disconnected. In that moment, not only was I feeling emotionally alone in a very busy situation, I had a sense of physical aloneness. I wasn't chasing children, fixing food plates, picking up toys and all the million other parental tasks that watching from the outside was exhausting enough. I didn't fit in and knowing I might never fit into that scenario was devastating.

I came to recognize that I often resented being in the situations I had been forcing for the sake of connection. This was a significant cause of why I felt so alone, despite so much going on around me and even for me. I even realized that I resented people, even my friends, in each of the places I had been, for not recognizing that I was in fact not having a good time, didn't fit in and yet carrying on with their busy lives, leaving me to figure it out for myself.

*"When we get too caught up in the busyness of the world, we lose connection with one another — and ourselves."*

—Jack Kornfield

It would have been very easy to throw a dart at a map, pack up a U-Haul and put thousands of miles behind me. However, for some reason, at that point in my life, I decided to give being alone a try right there in the place I was. I started doing the hikes I wanted to do. I started spending more time in my favorite place, Sedona, Arizona. I also started going to the movies alone. Doing what I wanted to do when I wanted to do it, had a refreshing sense of calm and power. This is not to mention the lack of energy it took to decide with no debate or comprising with others. I started volunteering with an equine therapy program, which ultimately was more therapeutic for me than I ever realized I needed. In fact, I could write an entire book on just how essential the horse and human connection is. I found all of these things enjoyable, refreshing, and fulfilling. However, I wished that I had someone to do those things with. It turns out that I'm pretty damn good company.

> *"Being alone has a power that very few people can handle."*
> – Steven Aitchinson

I also started traveling internationally. Being in a new country and not able to speak the language puts a whole new spin on alone in a busy world. However, this was a different kind of alone. I felt alive, open and inspired. Listening to and hearing my excited inner voice was an invaluable connection that I had previously not given true credit to. This was connecting on a brand new level.

Less than a year and a half after first traveling to Ecuador, a place I had fallen in love with and felt an unexplainable connection to, I was back on my third trip. This time I was living a love story! I was in an amazing place with someone I wanted to strengthen a connection with and falling in love with. However, there was a surprise! The person I was falling in love with, was ME. While I was with a beautiful, much younger man named Henry, salacious details best left for another chapter with a slightly more cautious parental rating, I was loving me. He was giving me the space to be my authentic self. I loved the way he made me feel, but ultimately I loved that I was allowing myself to have those feelings. These were feelings that were completely foreign to me. I had learned long ago that I wasn't loveable and, therefore, exerted an enormous amount of energy over the years, trying to find even an ounce of love. When I was telling my friends about the connection with this beautiful man, I was really telling them about the beautiful connection I had found with myself. The connection with this beautiful man will be a lifetime connection, since we created a life together. However, our time was meant to be no longer than the few days we did have together. It is a connection I am eternally grateful for, since he truly created the opportunity for the reintroduction of myself. I am holding out hope that I find that genuine kind of love I felt when I was with Henry, in another person who is meant for me.

And there it was. After all the years of feeling alone in a busy world, disconnected and unworthy, I was learning that to overcome the feeling of being alone in a busy world. I needed only to be my authentic self. I was now able to see that while I felt as if I were alone, which had been the reason for many of my own disconnections, I do, in fact, have some amazing, loving, and deep connections with amazing women. They are women who have been by my side for many years, listening to my discontentment in search of connections and loving me despite it. One of my deepest connections started when I was 10 years old. My dear friend Wendi and I met, just as my connection with my father was ending. As Wendi would say, "it was divine timing". Our connection was stronger than either of us knew, surviving several years of disconnection as we both navigated how to become an adult. Being my authentic self, loving myself and not trying so hard, helped me to not only recognize those connections but to honor them and show up as my best self for them.

All of these amazing women were absolute lifesavers, when I suffered the loss of the little soul I had created with Henry. A soul too beautiful for earth, who gained her wings before we could meet. The surprise of a natural pregnancy, after years of unsuccessful fertility assisted attempts at motherhood, rocked my foundation to the core and made me feel more alone than I have ever conceived possible. Yet each of these amazing women wrapped their love around me and without doubt, proved I have always had the love and connections I was so desperately seeking and chasing all over the world. Their love and strength gave me the will I needed to honor my own needs before anything else and take time off to recover from and grieve the loss. It took me several months to realize I needed to do so, as I took only two days off work following the loss and jumped right back into responsibility. I was still fearing the inevitable aloneness that was sure to accompany depression. During the two months I was away from work, I spent my time physically alone by choice. In that time, with a sense of self-connection and emotional strength of deep personal connections, I not only grieved the loss of my daughter, but also every other nasty emotion I had deeply buried and chosen to ignore rather than to face. This emotionally charged, raw, and ugly acknowledgment, acceptance and release of so many emotions had resoundingly positive results.

In honoring me, my connections and my desires, I am learning to attach to nothing and seek only that which is meant for me.

It may be scary at times and strange to others, but I am dancing with all that is meant for me, by living a want to live rather than a perceived have to life. Personal and shared connections are awakening with heartfelt truths and the promise of lifetime memories!

It is a busy world out there, but being loved for exactly who you are, provides a level of comfort that makes sometimes being alone, exactly as it should be.

# Rebecca Wright

Rebecca discovered, while feeling alone in a busy world and desperately seeking connections, that she is a connector. She often unknowingly inspires others to indulge in their interests and passions and has dedicated her time and career to helping others.

Rebecca is an experienced traveler. She does not like to sit still. Rebecca has visited and spent time in 42 of the 50 United States. She is looking forward to having visited all 50 states, before turning 50 years old. She has resided in seven states and each of the continental US time zones, including Alaska. After discovering a love of international travel, Ecuador quickly became a favorite and the most frequently visited. Rebecca's most recent trip to Ecuador was to volunteer with the Awaken Foundation, a program that provides a safe environment for youth impacted by incarceration. Her work with Awaken has continued beyond the time in Ecuador, since she is now providing administrative and fundraising support for the foundation.

Rebecca recently completed a second term with AmeriCorps. She first served as a VISTA (Volunteer in Service to America) in Great Falls, Montana with the Alliance For Youth, helping the community's vulnerable youth and families. Her most recent service as a State and National Volunteer was with the International Rescue Committee, providing financial literacy education to youth who have experienced foster care.

Rebecca earned a degree in criminal justice and spent several years working in law enforcement as a surveillance investigator. After transitioning to child welfare investigations, she was quickly promoted within the organization. Rebecca now works as a child welfare consultant and collaborates with various equine programs, including the Horses and Humans Research Foundation.

Rebecca enjoys sharing a kind and gentle smile with others and strives to be of service to others, while living an authentic life honoring connection.

Rebecca Wright
7455 N 95th Avenue #115
Glendale, AZ 85305
602-615-5774
starvista333@yahoo.com

# Megan Schwan

## *Overcome Anything*

Ah, life! Don't you just love how unexpected it is? For everyone, life is a journey. For some of us, it is a fight through the Amazon. My childhood was wonderful. I am the oldest of five, but I was loved and wanted for nothing. Starting in high school, things started changing. Trying to figure out who I was, I constantly forged my path without much of a thought and often to my detriment. Pregnant at 16, I was faced with a future that I had not planned for. I was responsible for someone other than me and faced with a decision to move forward through it or stay where I was.

It was scary, but I did somehow manage to move forward. I had a knack for accounting early on. When my teacher suggested that I make it a career, I went ahead and got my bachelor's. My daughter's father did not play a part in her life and so responsibility and challenges were often piled high on me. I thought my life was finally starting to look how I wanted, when I met and married my husband. We got pregnant with my second child and life seemed to finally be working in my favor. I had graduated and landed a decent full-time job. When I went on maternity leave, I decided not go back to work full-time. Instead, I got a job as a bookkeeper for a landscaping company. I would call this one of the sparkles of my life. I worked at that job and then my previous employer called me back to work part-time from home. I worked both of those jobs and thought things would improve. However, we were broke. It was timing-the-checking-account-to-clear-rent-before-bouncing-hamburger-helper-and-PB&J-all-the-time broke. We had made a bad move… literally. I still suffered from the people-pleasing syndrome and was trying to live up to an invisible standard, so we moved to a nice area outside of the city that was "expected" but outside of our price range. However, I made it happen and we made the move. It was a move that only lasted about a year. After that, we moved back to the city and eventually into a small two-bedroom apartment. Our bedroom was the living room and the kids were in each of the tiny rooms. Life was tough. It was a challenge trying to figure out what was next and take care of a family. I was not a homemaker. My Mom did an amazing job being one and well... I did not even pale in comparison.

This was when I started my business. The companies I was working for went through some changes and my position was ironically eliminated at both. I was stuck trying to figure out what to do next. I figured that since I had been working mostly from home as a bookkeeper, I could probably also do that for other companies. So, with a smidge of confidence under my belt and some direction, I started using social media to get my name out there. I slowly started building my business. I also got a part-time job to supplement my income, as I began growing my new business.

At this point, chaos felt like a pretty normal description for life. My perfect vision of what life would look like was non-existent. Marriage was hard, kids were hard, housekeeping was hard, adulting was hard and building a business was hard. Everywhere I looked, there was some kind of challenge that needed to be analyzed, solved and reconfigured. After two years in the business, I was finally starting to get a clue. I was working with a business coach, reading every recommended book and going to as many classes and networking events as I could stomach. I was getting to a point, where I needed to figure out what I was going to be doing next. Life was crazy, my business was growing and I was working part-time balancing work and family. How was I going to figure it all out!?

It was through more crazy, of course! I had finally decided that I could only put so much time into my business and work. I knew my business. I knew how to get clients. I also knew that if I spent the 20 hours while I was at work on growing my business, I would be able to supplement my income in no time. It was a leap and a calculated risk. However, I did it and haven't looked back since. However, this was also the exact moment my three-year-old son broke his femur. Crazy! I would never wish that on anyone. He endured seven weeks in a half-body cast over the summer. Thankfully, I was a week out from going into my business full- time, when my husband frantically called me at work. If you're not a spiritual person, that is okay. However, for me, I would not be able to make it through life without my God and my faith. This was one of those times that I was completely baffled and yet thankful for the timing. We made it through.

Fast forward to the next stage in life. It involved expanding our family and moving. We moved into a home and had our own space. If you've never been in a less than ideal apartment, you might not understand the complete relief you get from not having to hear other people live. I had also decided to hire a new employee for my expanding business and in preparation for having a new baby. Fast forward again and I had my wonderful third child and found out I was expecting again! Two babies in a year is a challenge in and of itself. My life has not stopped moving since. I also endured the challenge of an unexpected divorce and a shove back into single motherhood. My story in detail could probably fill a book by itself. However, this story has a take-away for your life. To recap, I've been a parent since before I was an adult. I went to college, got my degree, got a job, got married, had a baby, got laid off, started a business, moved to a crappy apartment, got another job, quit my job, my toddler broke his leg, moved, hired an employee, had another baby, separated-pending divorce, moved to a different city, had another baby (pregnant prior to separation), wait on divorce to finalize, COVID, still waiting on divorce, continued pandemic but… still made every day count.

I think one of the biggest challenges in life, is that we cannot control everything. Maybe it's just me and my personality, but I like control. I am an accountant. I like things to make sense and balance out. Ironically, my life has often looked like the opposite of balance and sense. However, I have figured out how to literally get through anything life or business throws at you. While the lessons to get to that point were hard to learn and are still evolving, they've made me better. I've learned a lot from my business, life and other people's stories.

If I had to summarize and pinpoint what I've learned in life so far it would be separated into four major lessons.

Lesson One. Control what you can. In business, we call it "Controlling the Controllables." In cliché, we call it the Serenity Prayer. However, in reality, it's true. You can only control you. You can't control how people will react or the dumb decision they will make that impacts your life or all the what-if scenarios which haven't happened. What you can control is you. This includes your reaction, your next step and your perspective. You CAN control you. While the world around you might be swirling and chaotic, you can choose what you will do and what you will focus on. Control what you can control.

Lesson Two. Find the Sparkles. One of my branding standout points in business from its inception, has been my shirts. I have always worn bedazzled logo shirts to events and networking. People recognize it and it sets me apart from the boring accountant norm I've never wanted to emulate. Sparkles are something I really enjoy. You should also strive for that perspective. What do I mean? In every situation and season, there is something good that can come out of it. We are all enduring this crazy pandemic and it has hit everyone differently. I can't help but also see many of the positive changes, evolutions and pivots that have also come from it. Life is often like that, which is okay. It is fine to feel two emotions at the same time and it is okay to have both bad and good come from the same situation. Finding the sparkles will help you get through anything life throws at you, because you cling to that small glimmer and eventually it gets bigger and bigger. If you haven't tried it, start today. Make a list if you have to! I promise with practice and consistency it will change your life, even if your circumstances don't change (see Lesson One). Life can always look one way from the outside but how life truly is for you, begins and ends with your own perspective. Find the Sparkle.

Lesson Three. Give Yourself a Break. I tell myself this so often, that it is practically my mantra. I was always the person who wanted to do things myself. I felt bad for quite some time about accepting offers to help. What an immature thing to do! I think having four kids, being a single Mom and a business owner changes this misconception, because the truth is that accepting offered help is amazing. Even more amazing, is giving yourself permission to not be perfect, to take the time off you need, to not expect everything to go right or always as planned, and not feel bad about it. Give yourself a break. This lesson is intertwined with all the lessons, because rest is vital to change. I think sometimes women have this struggle more than others. We hold ourselves or our thoughts at a high unattainable standard, which is ridiculous. Give yourself a break and then keep it moving!

Lesson Four. Learn the Lesson. I think this is a big one for personal growth. I heard someone once say that if you're not growing, you're dying. I think it was more about business. However, I think the same is true for life. If you want to achieve success and reach your goals, you have to be growing! Everything in life and business is a lesson, if you look for it. This differs from just finding the sparkles, because this is an action item. It's an action item because once you find the lesson, you have to also plan for the fix. This doesn't mean you won't make a similar mistake and end up in the same place. However, it does mean that you aren't going to sit and do nothing. Learn the lesson. Grow. Get Through.

The more I meet and talk to people and the more I read about super successful people and their journeys, the more these lessons solidify for me. Life is sometimes tough but it is malleable. You will have roadblocks, challenges, hang-ups and failures. However, you will also have joy, catapults, victories and conquests. The biggest factor towards ending up on the other side of it, is you. Once you can embrace who you are, see things differently and take control of what you can, you will be able to face everything else that comes next. Life is hard but it is beautiful. Don't give up! Step back, find the sparkle, take the break, learn the lesson and then run towards your success. If I can do it, so can you!

# Megan Schwan

Megan is the owner/operator of Sidekick Accounting Services. Discovering that she had a passion for accounting as a freshman in high school, she went on to graduate Cum Laude with her Bachelor's in Accounting from Liberty University in Lynchburg, VA. She started her first job in accounting at the age of 15 and has over 15 years of experience. She started Sidekick Accounting in 2014 and has since helped hundreds of small businesses organize and understand their numbers. Megan's family is the driving force behind her business, since she is the mother of four. When she is not working, she is usually exploring new things and places with her kids, enjoying the outdoors, reading a new book, or learning something fun. She knows how important a successful business is to a family and also wants every small business to be successful. Understanding and using your numbers accurately is key to running a successful business. Sidekick Accounting strives to help you get this organization, understanding and peace of mind, so your business succeeds and beats the statistic that 8 out of 10 small businesses fail.

Megan Schwan

Sidekick Accounting Services

111 E Wisconsin, Suite 301

Neenah, WI 54956

414-702-5012

Megan@Sidekick-Accounting.com

www.Sidekick-Accounting.com

# Karen Murray

## *Be Unstoppable With your Marathon Journey of Life and Reaching Your Financial Goals*

At age 44, I was a little overweight, with high cholesterol and glucose levels. The doctor prescribed exercise. Since I worked full-time and had three kids and a deaf mother at home, I decided that running would be the most convenient option. I wouldn't need a partner, a gym or any special equipment. I already had sneakers. So, I started to walk/run.

At first, it was mainly walking. However, I soon found myself running more than walking, and some weight came off. I was so psyched that I was getting fit, in 2010 when someone in my office said they would be doing a sprint triathlon and wanted to get a group of co-workers together, I said "Sure!" At the time, I couldn't even swim freestyle, which is standard (though not mandatory) in a triathlon.

I hadn't run when I was younger. I was born to deaf parents. My first language was American Sign Language. I learned English through the Sesame Street records that my parents played for me, so I could hear spoken language. I grew up faster than most children, since I had to interpret for my parents. When kids — and adults, too — saw my parents signing, they would ask me if my parents were "deaf and dumb." This is how they referred to deaf people in the 1970s. I always answered, "NO."

My mother and father were not generous people. They never praised me for my schoolwork or my hobbies. They never thanked me for interpreting for them from the age of three. It took me five decades to realize where my feelings of not being good enough came from and to understand my insecurity.

Naturally, they didn't encourage me to go to college. Therefore, I started working full-time at the age of 16. After High School, I soon realized the advantages of higher education, so I put myself through college at night. It took ten years, but I got it done, all while raising two children. When I graduated, I was pregnant with my third.

The whole time, my priority was my kids, my mom and my full-time job. I took care of others for over two decades. When my daughters graduated from high school and my son was a teenager, I started focusing on myself. Therefore, I signed up for that first-ever race, a triathlon with my co-workers. Unlike the fancy bikes that most triathletes rode, with their thin wheels made for speed, mine was a humble hybrid bicycle (a mix of a mountain and a road bike) with fatter wheels. Nonetheless, I was determined to finish a sprint triathlon. I was ridiculously confident, because I had never even had a two-hour workout. I just decided that I could do it!

I showed up on race day not knowing what a transition area was, nor a chip. I also couldn't find my colleagues. I was still able to swim the half-mile using the breaststroke (and getting some curious glances). I biked the 12 miles on my hybrid bike, which means I rode upright, and not leaning forward for speed as most of the others. What about running 5K or 3.1 miles at the end? Swimming and biking are very fatiguing! Therefore, I did a walk/run combo, which was all I could do at the time. When I crossed the finish line, my arms automatically went up in victory and they called my name, "Karen Murray!" I said to myself, "Hey, that's me!" I couldn't figure out how they knew my name — before I realized it was on my chip!

I finished! I've never been so proud of myself. It turned out that none of my co-workers even made it to the race that day. I emailed my bosses telling them I'd completed the triathlon. I used their mentor's phrase, "perseverance is genius in disguise," and they forwarded my email to the chairman of the company.

That was my first race. This was when my confidence started to bloom. I was so excited about finishing, that I signed up for 2 more sprint triathlons that summer. I also registered for swimming lessons. I figured there must be a reason why I was the only one swimming the breaststroke.

In 2011, I decided to up my game and try an Olympic distance triathlon (usually a .9 mile swim, a 26-mile bike, and a 10K finish). When I completed the Westchester Olympic Tri I, couldn't believe my feeling of accomplishment! However, I kept wanting more challenge. In 2012, I registered for my first half ironman (1.2-mile swim, 52-mile bike, and a half marathon finish). How in the world would I finish a half ironman, without having run a half marathon? I decided to join a local run group, the NewRo Runners, in New Rochelle, NY. Who would have thought that joining your local run club could change your life? These guys are so awesome! They were my supporters and cheerleaders!

My first half marathon was the Brooklyn Half in May 2012. Training and racing with the group made the miles go fast. I was having a lot of fun, and finished the race in 1:55:23. With a half marathon now under my belt, I had the confidence that I needed to finish the half ironman in August. I was also finally swimming freestyle!

After finishing the half ironman, the NewRo runners asked me to join them at the Wineglass Marathon in October 2012 in Corning, N.Y. I had never run a whole marathon before, but my friend Nina said all I needed to do was to "throw in a 19 miler." So, that's what I did.

I wound up inadvertently running with two friends, Mark and Julie. Nine miles in, I looked over at them and said, "I don't think I can keep this pace." They turned to me and said, "We're running to complete this marathon in sub 4." Little did I know that many recreational marathoners try running marathons in less than 4 hours. Until that moment, I had no idea that was their goal! They ran on ahead. This was my first marathon. I had no time goal, I only wanted to finish. I will never forget the beautiful countryside and the fall foliage. However, at mile 15, I came to a sudden halt. My legs cramped so much, I had to pull over and stretch. I didn't know anything about nutrition, hence the leg cramping. (I would now make sure to take enough electrolytes.) I didn't know many things about marathoning, but I always envisioned myself at that finish line. Quitting was NOT an option! I always knew I would finish, no matter what it took. That first time, it took four hours, thirty-four minutes, and twenty-eight seconds (4:34:28). I have never focused on being fast, only to finish. I didn't run a sub 4, until my 92nd marathon, when I decided it was time to qualify for the hard-to-enter Boston Marathon.

Like most marathoners, I was emotional crossing my very first finish line. I burst into tears. Thankfully, NewRo Runners had booked a hotel right there! I limped over to the hotel to get in the shower. I was scheduled to be at work the following day, a Monday, and I could hardly walk. So, this was a marathon? One and done! I never wanted to run another marathon again!

The pain was short-lived, like childbirth! Two weeks after I finished my first marathon, I decided I wanted to run another, so I could beat my Wineglass time. I signed up for the Philadelphia Marathon in November 2012. I did beat my time, and I felt so good! My running peers were there again to support me and cheer me on. Another runner friend (actually, an "accountability partner") and I decided that in 2013 we would run a half marathon or a marathon every month. We signed up for the San Diego Marathon, held in June 2013. Unfortunately, my runner friend had to cancel, due to a family emergency. I was still going to visit my dear friend Traci, who lived in San Diego. She turned out to be the best race concierge ever! At mile 3, I stepped into a hole in the road and fell. Although the blood was running down my leg, I was able to keep on running. The fall left a heart-shaped scar on my knee. I joke to this day that I left my heart in San Diego. Traci picked me up at the finish line, brought me to her house for an ice bath and cooked dinner for me. I was being cared for. It was awesome!

I started learning about different national run clubs: the Marathon Maniacs, the Half Fanatics, the 50 State Club, to name a few. That was when my pastime became an obsession! I decided I wanted to be a Marathon Maniac.

To enter the club, you need to either run two marathons within 16 days or three marathons within 90 days. I would try for the latter. I was able to get into Chicago through a lottery, I was already scheduled for the New York City Marathon and I would go back to run the Philadelphia Marathon again. After crossing the finish line of the Philadelphia Marathon in 2013, I was officially a marathon maniac.

In January 2014, my girlfriend Julia invited me to be her running bridesmaid at the Maui Marathon, where she was "maui'd". She then invited me to go with her the following month to Jacksonville, Florida, to race in Run for Donna, which supports breast cancer. I ran in memory of my Aunt Joyce, who had recently died of breast cancer. In March 2014, that same friend (can we still call her a friend?) invited me to the Shamrock Marathon in Virginia. Here I was at a marathon a month, in a few different states. I started thinking, Wouldn't it be great if I could do a marathon a month for all of 2014? Well, that quickly turned into, wouldn't it be great if I could run all 50 states before I turn 50? I figured it wasn't possible, both financially and logistically. However, in April 2014, I wound up doing three marathons in three different states in a one-week driving trip with my son during spring break. My run group was impressed that I ran three in one week! I don't think anyone in the club had ever done that. That was the first year they named me Runner of the Year.

I soon learned of a five-day series: five marathons in five days. I had to try that one! After that, I upped it again, with seven marathons in seven days. Long story short, three days before I turned 50, I'd finished a marathon in all 50 states. Lesson learned: Set your goal, say it out loud to the Universe and make it happen! Nothing is impossible, when you set your mind to do it!

When I'd completed my 50th state (Alaska), I had run 75 marathons. So, guess what that meant? Another goal! Where should I run my 100th marathon? I decided it would be really cool to return to my first marathon, five years later, and run my 100th marathon there. So, only one day after my 99th marathon in West Virginia, I returned to the Wineglass Marathon.

The journey continues. As of this writing, I've completed 191 marathons, which includes 19 ultras, or races longer than 26.2 miles, and I've never been healthier. No more high cholesterol or glucose, and I'm beating my family gene history of heart disease and diabetes.

Crossing so many finish lines has created a mindset of being UnStoppable. These life experiences have taught me so many lessons and how important planning is in every stage of life. I want to assist you with your planning and protecting you and your family on your marathon journey of life and being unstoppable in reaching your financial goals. From Protecting your Foundation, Growing Your Family to Enjoying Your Legacy. I will be with you every step, in whatever stage of the journey you are in and as your needs change:

- Life Insurance: Accidental Death; Mortgage protection; Term, Universal & Whole; Final Expense

- Health: Disability; Dental/Vision; Medicare Supplement; Long Term Care; Critical Illness

- Asset Management & Wealth Strategies: Debt Free Life; Annuities; Mortgage Acceleration; Everplans

My goal is to set a road plan for you to meet your financial goals! Check out all the offerings at https://karenbmurray.net/contact/

# Karen Murray

Karen is a mom to three. Karen has completed 191 marathons to date, including a marathon in every state. As of October 2020, she is currently working on the third round of running a marathon in every state, which requires a lot of planning. Karen has coached many people to meet their running and health goals. She is now working with families to protect what matters most through mortgage protection, retirement protection and a debt-free life. She's also recruiting for growing her agency. If you're looking for a career change where (i) people come first; (ii) you seek personal growth; (iii) integrity is honored; (iv) there is open communication; (v) you enjoy being of service and doing good in the world and (vi) you want to have fun and be productive, part-time or full-time, contact me so I can show you how to build your own business with unlimited opportunities and growth potential.

Karen Murray
Be Unstoppable With your Marathon Financial Plan
Symmetry Financial Group

405 Delancey Avenue
Mamaroneck, NY 10543

898 Mallory Road
Kents Store, VA 23084

203-918-7736
Karen@KarenBMurray.net
MurrayKaren621@gmail.com
https://KarenBMurray.net/contact/

# Dolores "MamaDuck" Allen
## *Orphanage Without Walls*

That large white building -- it loomed in the sky. At least, that's how I felt about it each time I passed it while riding the bus in Los Angeles on my way to somewhere. It strangely attracted my attention. I was about 9 or 10 when I first noticed it. While riding the bus I would lean over just enough to try to see the name on it. I was about 13 when I finally saw only a portion of the name…"Orphanage"! Perhaps, if things got worse, "when I run away, I could go there", I thought.

Looking back, at about the age of 9 or 10, I often watched the Shirley Temple Show I felt sorry for the kids that lived in those orphanages. They were dismal and so were the people who ran them. It really bothered me to the point that most of my young life I dreamed of owning an orphanage It would be cheerful, with bright walls and pretty bedspreads – girlie colors, etc. It would provide a loving environment, with positive discipline, a positive and caring staff and the warmth that adolescent girls need to develop healthfully. I wanted to visit the big white building one day….not just pass by it. I was hoping this one would be different.

As I reflected on my childhood, I felt that I was treated like an orphan. My mother did not choose to bond with me, only to dress me nicely with no emotional exchange. She was never a "go-to" mother, only a strict disciplinarian with changing moods. She was the "drill sergeant" in my life, to say the least. So, I had to self-nurture. I recall that I often said nice things to myself, like "you're a good girl".

The day arrived when I ran away. However, it was not from home! I was 18 and this was my first job. I became overwhelmed when Los Angeles County changed over to computers! I was employed as a Clerk Typist. When the computers arrived, I could not take it! My fear of what I didn't know about computers overtook me. I got up and walked off my job!

Working in a building right outside of downtown Los Angeles placed me a great distance from the location of a Bible tent meeting that I planned to attend that evening. I had a lot on my mind, so the walk was good therapy for me. As I walked, I stumbled upon that white building! I stood there in amazement daring to go up those steps. It was a foreboding decision! However, when I went to the counter and asked for a tour of the "orphanage," they told me they were not the orphanage. They were the corporate office! I was devastated as I managed to take my body out of that building and down the steps!

While I carried the dream of owning an orphanage throughout my life, an opportunity to develop a non-profit came my way.

Approaching the opportunity to found a girls' organization, however, left me with fear and trepidation. I did not visualize myself as a founder! Yet, the team of women who joined me in this vision insisted that I take the lead.

After the girls and leaders organized it, they named the church chapter, Sisters for Christ. They met at church twice a month. It became a Life Skills organization that addresses the multi-dimensional needs of girls ages 10-18. It promotes itself as a "safe place" nurturing organization and gives young girls the freedom to open up and discover themselves and their dreams. They learn to bond together in a positive manner and to network. The girls participate in a curriculum of life skills modules such as etiquette, leadership, career planning, financial management, community service, etc. with a volunteer dream team of women who are facilitators. This vision includes the slogan "Creating a Safe Place!" -- a safe forum -- emotionally, intellectually and mentally. The primary focus: building from the "inside out" – reaching the true innate beauty of each individual while developing their self-esteem. In 2004, we became a nonprofit. We named it Sisters In Sync, Inc. (SIS, Inc.)

From 2002 to 2011, after participating in the modules and field trips for nine months, the leaders and girls participated in a formal awards banquet each spring. It was a grand occasion. It honored the girls, the leaders, and parents with awards of Commitment, Sister of the Year, Parent of the Year, Leadership, Caring Heart (Community Service), Senior Cotillion, Dedication of New Members, etc.. Their parents and guardians as well as supportive friends attended each year. The girls were able to practice what they learned about social etiquette! The "tomboys" practiced walking in their "ten-minute" high heeled shoes! It was held in gorgeous ballrooms.

Even though we received a few donations from private donors, I contributed the majority of financial support. The market of corporations who were contributors was attracted to well-established non-profits. We were the new kids on the block!

We also established the Sharyse Napue Memorial Scholarship Fund for senior girls who were members and met the criteria. Sharyse was a cherished charter member of Sisters for Christ who died unexpectedly.

SIS, Inc was working well with the volunteer dream team. They were committed to using their talents and skills to assist in their development. We were an awesome team. In 2012, we changed the aka under SIS, Inc. from *Sisters for Christ to My Sister My Friend.*

"So what! We don't have money!", I thought. SIS, Inc. needed material resources to sustain it. It needed a Teacher's Manual, a Curriculum, and a Girls' Workbook . The dream team asked me to write it. That request took me out of my comfort zone but I consented. I'd never written anything of this magnitude! I named the resources, the "Safe Place Kit".

This was the first point at which I felt *unstoppable*! It was God Who whispered in my heart that SIS, Inc. IS THE WHITE BUILDING. "Where is the orphanage I wanted?" I asked. He said, "You have an orphanage without walls!" How awesome is God!

And then it happened.

One morning I woke up with a throbbing headache. This was most unusual. On the night of May 30, 2012, at the request of my daughter-in-love, Tania, my son Damon drove me to Bowie Clinic. I was diagnosed with a subdural hematoma and driven by ambulance to George Washington University (GWU) hospital for emergency surgery for removal of the blood clots on the left side of my brain. I remained in the hospital for three days and then was released.

I recovered well. At least I thought so. After about a week and a half, I returned to GWU hospital with brain hemorrhaging. I was placed in ICU after four hours of surgery and then in the Critical Care Unit. It left me paralyzed on my right side, with no memory and unable to speak or eat. I did not know who I was or anyone else! That lasted over two weeks, after which I "woke up"!

It was during the plans for my transportation to the Medstar National Rehabilitation Center (NRC) were being discussed, I recall hearing voices from their medical transportation staff. Mind you, I did not know that I'd had major brain surgery nor that I was paralyzed and couldn't speak. I didn't know I was leaving GWU Hospital. My brain just allowed me to accept whatever was happening to me at the time. I looked down at my right hand. It looked flat and I could not move it, but my brain did not allow me to think it was abnormal—even paralyzed! I had no questions of why I was on that bed, being wheeled out. None!

That Thursday, my family helped me set up residence at the NRC, and visited, nurtured, and cared for me every day. They were the positive influence in my blessed recovery. They posted family pictures, brought balloons, plants, cards…! They brought me smoothies, food, and my favorite ice cream. They propped me up, fed me, cleaned out my mouth when I held food, and prayed for me.

The next day, Friday, my therapy did not go well. My kind therapist gently placed me in the wheelchair, put a belt around me, and took me out to their massive gymnasium of therapeutic apparatus. She pulled me up by the belt and held it as she had me walk the bars. They later told my family I may never be ready for their therapy. The very next day, Saturday, I felt awesome energy going through my body. When I walked the bars, the therapists teased me saying, "Who is this?" I had done exceptionally well! My progress increased with PT, OT and Speech Therapy. Eventually, I began to say words!

I was discharged on July 17, 2012, and went to my son's home to recuperate. The spoiling from my daughter Trisha, daughter-in-love Tania, and grandchildren continued. Yet, despite the amenities and support, I struggled with a monster, Thanatophobia, *the fear of dying*. It came to me at night before I went to sleep, or it woke me up in the middle of the night. It was the deep dark fear of the unknown. It was the fear of the sharp feelings in my head and realizing that I had been delivered from death and permanent paralysis. Being alive frightened me because I wondered every day if I would die or have to repeat what I'd gone through. I knew that I had to get through this because I believed that this fear wanted to destroy me and all the good that God had already done and would do for me.

My research taught me there are many types of fear. Phillip Puff, PhD., Licensed Clinical Psychologist, of *Psychology Today* says, "Fears are thoughts that we have created usually after having a negative experience. I say "usually" because fears cannot only come from our own experiences but also from those of others. We experience a negative event and we reinforce the fear by thinking about it and analyzing its negative impact on our lives. Thus fears are created, perpetuated, and sustained in our minds."

*How Fear Works* by Julia Layton shares with us that "Fear is a chain reaction in the brain that starts with a stressful stimulus and ends with the release of chemicals that cause a racing heart, fast breathing, and energized muscles."

Since there are a variety of fears that can affect those of us who have survived a brain injury, you may want to find a professional with training and experience to help you through your fears. I did not have the financial ability to do that. However, I learned that meditation is a positive cure for the fear of dying. So, I turned to my Bible.

One morning, I noticed my Bible was open to Jeremiah 30:17: "For I will restore health to you and heal you of your wounds, says the LORD." This scripture spoke life to my heart and mind. I embraced those words! Whenever the weird feelings shot through my head I held God to His promise. I had the hope I needed! What a miracle!

After five months of outpatient therapy with Medstar, I was able to drive myself home which is approximately a 110-mile trip I was excited that I could begin work again on the "Safe Place Kit'! Creating this course of three resources has been a great source of purpose and fulfillment. After nine years (and despite Covid-19), I have finally completed editing the manuscripts and have transferred them to the designer!

"…I'll show up and take care of you as I promised and bring you back home. I know what I am doing. I have it all planned out. Plans to take care of you, not to abandon you, plans to give you the future you hoped for." Jeremiah 29: 10-11- *Message*

**Dolores "MamaDuck" Allen**

Dolores "MamaDuck" Allen is the mother of three grown children and the grandmother of four. She is a retired Administrative Assistant and a Certified Youth Trainer (CYT), who resides in beautiful Hancock, Maryland. She is a survivor of a subdural hematoma, and, in her "new normal", has continued to follow her dream of creating a curriculum of life skills resources for girls. She founded a nonprofit, "Sisters In Sync, Inc. (SIS, Inc.) At present, the resources are *being designed.*

The *My Sister My Friend Safe Place Kit* consists of:

**MSMF Teachers' Manual** — This manual contains information and guidance for the teacher. It gives clarity to the concept of "Creating a Safe Place!" as she conducts her classes for girls who desperately need to get connected with themselves and others in a safe environment.

**MSMF Curriculum** — contains a variety of the modules and activities that provide introspection to girls from 8th grade to 12th grade. They are exposed to the positive life skills necessary for multi-dimensional growth and development.

*MSMF All About Me Girls' Workbook* — This comprehensive workbook contains the modules and activities that comprise the "Safe Place" concept. It supports a positive value system, while it focuses primarily on the needs of cross-cultural girls from grades 8th to 12th.

**The** *My Sister My Friend Safe Place Kit* is an answer to the need for a purpose-driven life skills school course, as well as a solution to the great need for training young girls to be Christian leaders.

Dolores thanks' God for the powerful grace and peace He gave her, when her heart was anxious; and His faithful "promises," when fear for her future overwhelmed her.


Dolores "MamaDuck" Allen
Sisters In Sync, Inc.
8905 Slabtown Road
Hancock, MD 21750
301-213-0601
sisinc2002@gmail.com
www.sisnsyncinc.org

# Wendi Wiltfang

## *Imperfect and Free from My Own Rules*

*"It is better to live your own destiny imperfectly than to live an imitation of somebody else's life with perfection."*

—The Bhagavad Gita

**Imperfect and Free From My Own Rules**

It was July 30, 2006. I had just turned 30, which was my golden birthday. I celebrated by throwing myself a huge catered, open bar, 80's themed costume birthday party for 150 of my friends and family that cost around $5,000. I was living large and wanted to celebrate. I wore a prom queen tiara and a custom black 80's style prom dress. I had been married to my high school sweetheart for 10 years. We had our daughter Claire, who was almost three. I was busy selling real estate and had finally earned my goal of over $100,000 in a single year in 2005 and was on that same track for 2006. We vacationed at Disney World once or twice a year. Life appeared to be good.

My friend since elementary school, Becky, had flown in to be at my birthday party. She and I had kept in close touch since high school and I knew that things were not going great in her life. She planned to come back to Indiana around her birthday, towards the end of August. As a gift for her, I found a local tarot card reader and made us both appointments.

It was a Saturday night and when we knocked on the door of the small house, we were greeted by a pretty young lady, named Vanessa, who I had guessed was younger than us. Before she began, she mentioned that if she felt we needed to have our readings separately that she would tell us. We agreed.

Becky and I had decided that she would go first. In my mind, I was just there to support her. I had never had a tarot card reading before and my life was basically "perfect". What did I need a reading for? It was all about my friend and her hopefully seeing some positive changes coming in her future. Either way, it would be a fun experience for Becky and me to have together for our birthdays.

We all sat down. Vanessa began to shuffle the cards and had Becky pick some. I sat quietly next to her, while Vanessa brought up many things that definitely seemed to apply to Becky's life and family, past and present. I was shocked. Becky kept looking at me, wondering if I had somehow told Vanessa things ahead of time about her. I said I hadn't. Many of the things I didn't even know. Becky got her reading and some good insights about what was going on and coming in her future.

Vanessa looked at me and said she would like to do my reading in private. Becky and I looked at each other suspiciously and then I agreed.

Vanessa took me back to a bedroom where she had another table set up. After I selected my cards, she started my reading. She began by telling me there was someone in my life that I tried really hard to be perfect for. Someone who I overachieved for, in order to win their love and acceptance.

I immediately knew that she was wrong. My mom and my grandparents accepted me no matter what. No one had pushed me to overachieve or to be perfect. I knew that I could do a little or a lot and they would love and accept me all the same.

I argued with her that it wasn't me. There was no one in my life fitting that description. I knew I couldn't explain where the drive that I had to excel in school, work, and life came from. However, I knew for certain it wasn't from any of them. We agreed to disagree, and she moved on.

When I had called in to make our appointments, she said to bring any items that we wanted her to try to get any energy or messages off of. I had remembered and grabbed my great grandma's wedding band on my way out the door.

I handed her this wedding band. She held it close to her chest, took a deep breath, and said, 'This is it. Whoever this ring belongs to, is who I'm talking about. It is someone who you have always pushed yourself to be better and perfect for and to be loved and accepted by."

Stunned, I felt a large missing puzzle piece fall into place in my mind and body. It was clear. It was true. When I was young, I lived most of my childhood with my grandparents. My grandma's mother also lived with us. She was my great grandma Beck. To spend time with her in her living room downstairs, playing games, doing puzzles and watching her TV programs, I had to behave...perfectly. There were no exceptions. If I acted up, I had to leave and go upstairs and leave her alone. She had zero tolerance for goofing off. The mystery was solved. She was the reason why I've always pushed myself harder and further. Due to her influence, I always expected perfection of myself and others. I followed all of my made-up rules and expected others to follow them as well. There was an explanation. Wow. I had an "I MAY NOT BE CRAZY MOMENT." I had been subconsciously trying to please her all of those years in every area of my life. I would always do "the right thing". I would tattle on others, if they didn't do "the right thing". I would be a good girl to ultimately win the approval of someone who passed away, when I was 11 years old.

Vanessa then added "Wendi, you have been putting on a show for people. You strive for perfection. You keep taking all of these classes. You read all of these books. You are controlling and you have made up rules for yourself and for others to follow. You put the weight of the world on your shoulders and you are miserable. You are exhausted."

By this time, I was full-on bawling. This girl had seen right through me and called me out with kindness. I had always fooled everyone else with my "show". I felt vulnerable. I wanted to run back to life, before I walked in that front door. However, could I truly argue with her and what she was saying? I remembered that I had been told by someone close to me that people walked on eggshells around me. Which I'm sure they did. When I'm expecting perfection and being controlling, there was no winning with me. Therefore, maybe what she was saying was true. Thankfully, she was soft and gentle and she continued...

"You've been looking and looking and what you are really looking for is God. And the peace of God."

I felt something shift. I trusted her. She had given me information that had made me feel better. When she invited me to learn about and experience peace, I surrendered and said: "I don't know what you are talking about, but I want it."

This was the first time in my life that a teacher, coach, or mentor wasn't telling me to push myself to do more, read more, learn more, sell more or be more. She was telling me to simply sit quietly and breathe for a few minutes once a day. She asked me to stop reading self-help books or going to classes for a while. I was being taught about meditation, except we didn't use that word and I was instructed not to google it or do any research on it. She knew I would just overcomplicate it. This was exactly the guidance I needed at that time.

I spent the next few years working with Vanessa and learning about God and the peace that is available to all of us. She taught me how to be open to communication with God. I was open to learning about the idea that any specific conversation or story about something that happened in my past could affect my thoughts and actions negatively into my entire future. Gaining access to this shifted the whole way I saw life and how I interacted with people, especially in my most important relationships.

God was getting me prepared for what was coming. Four short years later, I would be divorcing, declaring bankruptcy, sharing custody of Claire and living back in my old high school bedroom at my Mom's house. My personal life also took a toll on my business and my sales dropped. I further shattered the illusion of being perfect publicly. I was no longer a good girl who always did the right thing by causing the divorce. I was not perfect, and my secret was out. Somehow as awful as that time was, I had never felt freer and more honest with myself.

As I continued to do this work, I recalled a situation from elementary school. After a disappointing interaction where a group of girls, one of whom I considered to be my best friend, said I couldn't sit with them at lunch anymore. I subconsciously decided to never have a best friend and to protect the other kids from that group. In hindsight, what actually happened was I became a bully to this group of girls. I believed that I was protecting others from being betrayed, like I believed they had betrayed me.

It was becoming obvious that I had created many rules in my life. One day at 38, I realized that I was carrying around rules I had made up at the age of 15 around having sex. A friend helped me to realize that although those rules served me well at 15 and kept me safe and not pregnant, those rules no longer supported the types of adult relationships I was having. This realization led me to understand the judgment I had of myself and others as it related to sex.

With this realization and more to come, I became open to asking for coaching around anything that wasn't working in my life. I learned that I had the following contradicting, paralyzing beliefs running subconsciously. I believed that I wasn't good enough and couldn't be successful, unless I was with a man. If I was single or not in a committed relationship, I couldn't be successful. On a deeper level, this made me feel as if I was a failure. Ouch.

Because of these beliefs, I had been punishing myself for years with the way I was dating. I was holding myself back and not making as much money as I was capable of. I was waiting for a man to build businesses with me, instead of building one on my own. I was the Master of Self Sabotage. Once I became aware of this thinking and how it related to the rules I had established in my younger years, I was free to behave differently in my relationships and to build a business for myself.

I'm a few weeks past the deadline and even as I write these words, my old friend, Perfection, is right beside me, looking over my shoulder. It doesn't disappear. It just doesn't run my life these days. I feel the fear and have the urge to run from my commitments. I recognize it. I feel the desire to be perfect and thank it for its contribution to my life. I take a deep breath and step forward with an open and surrendered heart. The illusions of being perfect or in control can be exhausting. I let go of getting it right, being perfect, looking good and putting on a show. I'm no longer pretending to be in control of anything. My fears about someone seeing my vulnerability almost cost me my dreams. I don't know what my future holds, but I do know I'm committed to this amazing life I'm creating. And it's definitely not perfect.

*"And the day came when the risk to remain tight in a bud was more painful than the risk it took to blossom."*

—Anais Nin

# Wendi Wiltfang

Wendi is an unstoppable force of kindness, love, acceptance and support for those around her. She loves spending time with her beautiful daughter, Claire, her adorable, three-year-old, ball of energy, nephew, Jace and her rat terrier puppies, Bailey and Abbey. For over 22 years, Wendi has helped hundreds of people buy and sell their homes in Northwest Indiana as a real estate broker. After years of being committed to lifting, elevating and inspiring others, the time came to create her own wellness practice. Wendi will be helping people thru multiple modalities, including reiki, reconnective healing and setting intentions for her clients to experience more peace and freedom in their lives. She is always looking to celebrate and empower those around her, by recognizing and acknowledging their beauty, worthiness and growth and becoming who they want to be. Wendi is always packed and ready for frequent road trips to places like Chicago, St. Louis, Mackinac Island, Lake of the

Ozarks, Nashville, Phoenix and Sedona. Her love of travel started during her childhood, while exploring the western United States with her grandparents. Summers always started with a road trip to visit family in Oklahoma, then continued west from there. Her grandfather, Wayne, is a famous western artist. They have visited places like Breckinridge, Yellowstone, Jackson Hole, Flagstaff, Albuquerque, Taos, Santa Fe, then back to Oklahoma stopping at galleries and scenic places for him to paint. Visit Wayne Cooper Art Gallery on Facebook. Coming in the spring of 2021 is "We Sister So Hard," a collaboration with her sister, Tawni. This project will include a blog, podcast, book and multiple events starting in Northwest Indiana. It will share their sisterly adventures growing up together and overcoming some of the common issues sisters may come across, including the good, the bad and the ugly with their ultimate triumph of becoming great friends.

Wendi Wiltfang
126 W 1025 S
Kouts, IN 46347
219-405-3595
ValpoRealtor@gmail.com

Making an Impact, One Story at a Time!

www.OvercomingMediocrityPodcast.com